Voices from Within
Women Who Have Broken the Law

EVELYN K. SOMMERS

Foreword by Paula J. Caplan

Women in conflict with the law have their own ideas about why and how they became lawbreakers. But the experts who tell us who these women are and why they break the law usually ignore or discredit outright the opinions of the women themselves.

As a counselling and research intern in a women's medium-security prison, Evelyn Sommers heard the stories of dozens of women inmates who came for counselling. Their crimes involved prostitution, drug abuse, theft, physical abuse, assault, and arson. Their stories called into question existing theoretical explanations for criminal behaviour as well as the explanations commonly heard in the day-to-day discourse of the prison. Sommers concluded that attempts to help women lawbreakers could be effective only if they took into account the women's understanding of what led to their lawbreaking. She resolved to conduct intensive interviews with fourteen women and to look for the common threads in their stories – threads that might further our understanding of women's conflicts with the law.

Sommers presents the women's accounts without excusing or condemning them, and without moulding their explanations to some ideological model. The four common threads that emerged from the women's accounts were need, disconnection and the influence of others, visible anger, and fear. Further analysis revealed two implicit, underlying themes: the centrality of relationships in the women's lives and their personal quest for empowerment. *Voices from Within* demonstrates the importance of conducting separate studies of male and female lawbreakers; of relying on subjective perspective to distinguish and appropriately address differences inherent in the criminal population; and of reconceptualizing the notion of criminal motivation. Sommers concludes with suggestions for further research and for practical approaches to working with lawbreakers.

EVELYN K. SOMMERS is a psychologist in private practice in British Columbia.

Voices from Within

Women Who Have Broken the Law

EVELYN K. SOMMERS

UNIVERSITY OF TORONTO PRESS
Toronto Buffalo London

© University of Toronto Press Incorporated 1995
Toronto Buffalo London
Printed in Canada

ISBN 0-8020-2998-1 (cloth)
ISBN 0-8020-7449-9 (paper)

Printed on acid-free paper

Canadian Cataloguing in Publication Data

Sommers, Evelyn K. (Evelyn Kathleen)
   Voices from within : women who have broken the law

   Includes bibliographical references and index.
   ISBN 0-8020-2998-1 (bound)   ISBN 0-8020-7449-9 (pbk.)

   1. Female offenders – Case studies. I. Title.

HV6046.S65 1995   364.3'74   C94-932256-3

University of Toronto Press acknowledges the financial assistance to its
publishing program of the Canada Council and the Ontario Arts Council.

This book has been published with the help of a grant from the Social
Science Federation of Canada using funds provided by the Social Sciences
and Humanities Research Council of Canada.

To fourteen women who wanted to be heard

Contents

Foreword

Like most people, I preferred to keep my distance from women prisoners – in fact, I preferred to avoid even thinking about them. Denying the shared humanity between ourselves and those who are marginalized as women prisoners is one of the ways we maintain a feeling of our own specialness or goodness. Evelyn Sommers plunges in and gets close to fourteen women prisoners, inspiring us to take a deep breath and take that plunge ourselves, if only in our minds and imaginations as we read this book. We don't know what we shall feel as we pass through the doorway of this book, for, as Adrienne Rich said in her poem 'Prospective Immigrants, Please Note,' 'The door itself makes no promises. It is only a door' (*Snapshots of a Daughter-in-Law: Poems, 1954–1962* [New York: W.W. Norton, 1967], p. 59).

Common images of women prisoners are of women far angrier than ourselves, more easily led than ourselves, with lower moral standards than our own. Often, women in prisons are assumed to lack intelligence: 'If they're so smart, why did they get caught?' Sommers begins with the disturbing but accurate observation that 'Women are rarely credited with having any real knowledge, even [or especially, one might add] knowledge of themselves. People in conflict with the law are rarely granted credibility. On these two counts, female lawbreakers have been silenced' (p. 3). This book changes all that, conveying to us the voices of a variety of imprisoned women, making sure we know how, and *that*, they think and feel.

Until now, women in prisons have been rendered invisible, distorted, or masked – invisible, because they have been ignored by criminality researchers; distorted, because they have been squeezed to fit into researchers' and theorists' descriptions of male prisoners; and masked, because who they are has been blotted out by researchers focusing on men in prisons or researchers who had no interest in really hearing women's descriptions of their lives.

With keen perceptions and thoughts, as well as a palpable sense of connection with the humanity of these women, a humanity we should be ashamed ever to have doubted, Sommers paves the way for a more productive understanding of how and why women break the law. Drawing on important feminist theory, she summarizes and carefully interprets the women prisoners' stories in ways that make enormous sense and that, in many ways, echo the experiences of most women.

Making sense but without making excuses for the women, trying as much as possible to walk in the shoes of those she interviewed, Sommers describes what the women feel led to their being imprisoned. Sommers' approach to the material and her attitude towards the women are models for researchers. She takes great care in interpreting the women's words and is straightforward about her decision to take a different approach from the one psychologists commonly take, of trying to ape natural sciences research. Confronting the dilemma of what to do when an interviewee seemed not to be telling the truth, Sommers modifies her methodology to give the woman the benefit of the doubt while maintaining the rigour of the study.

Sommers' work is informed by her subtly textured, feminist comprehension of the ways in which oppression in the form of sexism and, often, of racism and classism has made women feel powerless, isolated, and bereft, embedded in emotional isolation. She deals not only with the experiences of the individual women – and the continuing mystery of individual differences – but also with their social context. The result is a multidimensional picture of the women's lives and their routes to lawbreaking that leads to the productive rethinking of old theories and claims. The book provides future researchers with a gold-mine of avenues to explore, and contemporary clinicians and anyone who works with women in prisons will find the recommendations section in the last chapter full of suggestions that are to the point, practical, and sparkling with insight and humanity.

PAULA J. CAPLAN
April 1994

Acknowledgments

I wish to thank the following for their important contributions to this research: Adam Revesz, my son, for believing in me and for helping me learn invaluable lessons about parenting; Katherine Sommers, my mother, for showing me what courage and determination are all about; Wesley Sommers, my father, who shared his enthusiasm for learning in his chosen field; Paula Caplan, for her guidance through the original research and for being available to boost my spirit whenever I needed her; Barbara Burnaby, for her sound advice on methodological and ethical issues; Niva Piran, for her thoughtful insights concerning the research process; Marg Malone, for being available as a sounding board and support; Joanna Holt Oetke, Cindy Brooks, and Andrea Toepell, for their enthusiasm and feedback; Leigh Cross, for his editorial comments, his computer expertise, and for caring about this work; Dale Butterill and Valerie Gibson, for their comments on the original manuscript; all the friends and family members who encouraged me through the process; Liz Bolger, for suggesting that I'd be interested in working with female inmates; Gale Bildfell, for sharing her knowledge of women who have suffered the loss of stillbirth or miscarriage; all my supervisors and colleagues who have helped me learn how to hear; Alma Swetman and her nursing staff, Suzanne Tuzlak, Verna Nutbrown, and Roma Carlin, who provided me with on-site support; Levan Turner, for sharing his views; Paul Birmingham, for sharing his knowledge of computer programs; Shelley Gorman and Grant Coulson, for advocating for my internship in the prison; Darlene Zeleney, for her careful editing; Virgil Duff, Executive Editor of the University of Toronto Press, for his quick and encouraging response to the work; the Social Sciences and Humanities Research Council of Canada; and the Ontario Ministry of Correctional Services.

Voices from Within

Women Who Have Broken the Law

1

Women Knowing; Knowing Women

Women in conflict with the law have their own ideas about why and how they became lawbreakers. They've lived through the experience of law-breaking, and they know about it.[1] They have survived wrenching situations in which they were moved to act in ways that they sometimes angrily justify and sometimes profoundly regret. They have struggled with the social systems and structures that turn them from lawbreakers into criminals.[2] They face the reality of who they are as individuals every time they look into the mirror.

Women are rarely credited with having any real knowledge, even knowledge of themselves.[3] People in conflict with the law are rarely granted credibility. On these two counts, female lawbreakers have been silenced. Experts tell us who these women are and why they break the law, while the opinions of the women themselves are usually ignored or discredited outright. If we are to get to the bottom of women's conflicts with the law, we must go to the real 'experts.' We must listen to women like Marianne* and Connie, who were determined to maintain a decent standard of living for themselves and their children after separation from their husbands; like Jacqueline, who believed that the only way she could be accepted by her family was to provide them with expensive gifts; and like Vicki, who felt rejected by a mother and a grandmother in a culture characterized by separation and expression of pain through violence. We must take in the stories of women like Doreen and Lynne, who experi-

---

* All the names used in this book are pseudonyms. Details of the women's lives and cases have been altered, carefully, to protect the women while maintaining the integrity of the material.

enced and witnessed unspeakable violence, and like Doris, who spent most of her life in institutions.

As a counselling and research intern in a women's medium-security prison, I heard the stories of dozens of women who came for counselling. Their stories called into question the theoretical explanations for criminal behaviour contained in the literature as well as the explanations that I heard in the day-to-day discourse of the prison. As a counsellor, I had learned the value of uncovering and building upon the subjective experience of the individual; I deduced that attempts to help women in conflict with the law could be effective only if they were directed from a base of the women's understanding of what had happened to them. My plan, then, was to interview several women intensively and find the common threads in their stories that might be useful in understanding and addressing their conflicts with the law.

CONNECTING TO LEARN

Finding the aforementioned women and the seven others whose stories form the core of this book, and then hearing what they had to say, meant that I had to work within the constraints of their unchosen but then-current milieu. I selected the fourteen through a procedure I established after becoming familiar with the routines and culture of the prison. I learned that, as the women become acquainted with prison life, they gravitate into groups. A stratified subculture develops, with more powerful groups, or 'heavies,' influencing and intimidating the less aggressive groups. To avoid creating a situation in which the women might pressure each other either to participate or not to participate in the interviews, I approached women soon after they were admitted into the prison. I followed this guideline throughout the project to ensure procedural consistency, but soon realized that many of the women had already met at holding centres prior to their admission to the prison, and that some had been long-time friends or acquaintances. These meetings and alliances may have affected some of the women's decisions to participate in the research, but the extent of the effect remains unclear. However, I had no reason to believe that any women were pressured to volunteer.

The process of finding participants involved meeting for orientation sessions with small groups of inmates who were new to the prison. In the sessions I described my work, tried to uncover and dispel any fears the women had about participating in research interviews, and asked for their help. All the women who attended the orientation sessions completed a

form on which they indicated whether they agreed or declined to partic-
·ipate. The use of an individual form for each of the women meant that
volunteers could keep their intentions private. (See Appendix A for more
information about the method.)

The women's responses to my information and request ranged from
none at all to suspicion – 'Why should we trust you? You just walked into
the room and we've never seen you before' – to gratitude – 'I've been
waiting a long time for a chance like this.' Some were concerned about
what benefit they might realize through their participation and were satisfied when I said I hoped they might come to a better understanding of
themselves. Others said they'd like to be interviewed because their story
might help someone else.

In response to the expressions of mistrust, I simply agreed that the
women had no historical reason to trust me. I suggested that they follow
their 'gut' reactions to me and to what I was saying, and that they ask
questions, which some did.

Later, I selected five of the women who had refused to participate and
asked them why they had declined. Two said they didn't want to be 'used'
and one of these expressed a suspicion of 'psychologists.' One woman
made an association between me and 'all social workers'; she'd been un-
happy with the way she'd been treated by one on the 'outside.' One
woman said she didn't appreciate being called in to discuss her reasons
for not wishing to participate, told me that she didn't feel like talking
'now or ever,' and abruptly left the room. The fifth woman had been
concerned about the reaction of the other women attending the orientation meeting and, when reassured that they would not have to know of
her participation, offered to participate.

Of forty-four women who attended the orientation session, twenty-
seven volunteered. Another three indicated that they would have agreed
to participate had they expected to be in the institution long enough to
accommodate the interviews. The fourteen women I interviewed were selected according to age, race, number of times incarcerated, and type of
offence, for as wide a range of these criteria as possible.[4]

The women ranged in age from 19 to 48. They were born in both rural
and urban settings within the province, in other provinces, and in other
countries. The women's education levels ranged from no formal education
to Grade 12, and most said they had completed all or part of Grade 9.
All but three had been charged and sentenced previously. Nine of the
women appeared to be Caucasian; six of the nine confirmed this but two
had been adopted and didn't know their exact racial background. Three

of the women were Black, one was Métis, and one was Native. There were no East Indian or Asian women in the sample, a reflection of the small numbers of such women in the institution. There were French-speaking women in the prison, however, and two of the women interviewed – Danielle and Doris – both spoke French. Since they also spoke English, language was not a barrier, and I was able to draw upon the experiences of the two francophone women.

The distribution of racial or ethnic groups in institutions within the provincial and federal penal systems often depends on the kinds of charges typically laid against a particular group or on allowances made for women to serve their sentences in detention centres closer to their homes. For example, although official records regarding the race of women admitted were unavailable from the institution at which I carried out the research, it was my impression that there were far fewer Native women in the institution at the time of the research than has been estimated for Ontario, in general, by author Carol LaPrairie: she states that 17 per cent of women incarcerated in Ontario are Natives.[5] Data from the Ontario Ministry of Correctional Services for fiscal year 1989–90 indicate that 56 per cent of Natives sentenced (both female and male) were sentenced for default of fines, compared with 28 per cent of all sentenced individuals. Because such sentences are normally short, they are likely to be served in local jails, close to the homes of the women. This factor may account in part for the relatively small proportion of Native women in the institution used in this research, which is located far from any major concentrations of Native population. Moreover, the particular mix of the inmate population at a given institution may be the product of any of a number of other factors at play within the judicial and/or correctional systems. Thus, in this, as in any research, the pool of potential participants was a function of the time period and location of the study.

With the exception of Vicki, I interviewed each woman four times. Vicki's first language was her Aboriginal language, and she and I were both somewhat frustrated because I had difficulty understanding her and frequently asked her to repeat herself. To further complicate the process, just prior to our third interview, she was told that she would be leaving the prison in a few days. Vicki reacted to the news of her imminent release as many women do, with a great deal of anxiety. Given these complications, she decided to terminate her participation in the research after the third interview. None the less, her contribution stands as a valuable part of the study.

The interviews ranged in length from thirty minutes to two hours, but usually lasted one hour. They were scheduled weekly to allow for the development, over time, of trust and rapport, which enabled the women to share intimate details of their lives or to opt out of the research process if they wished to do so (none did). By scheduling the interviews on a weekly basis, I allowed ample opportunity for validation of the material through repetition and spontaneous confirmation of details. The interviews began with an open-ended question – 'Why do you think you broke the law?' – and then followed the women's train of response.[6] My probes usually took the form of pursuing the meaning of the women's statements, or looking further at a particularly emotional piece of information.

Even with the best of planning and intentions, listening was not something that happened easily in the prison. I interviewed the women in an office in the medical area of the prison, which, like the remainder of the complex, was constructed of concrete block. It had previously been a cell; floors were uncarpeted and the window was bare. Activity in the surrounding area created noise that would render parts of the audiotapes unintelligible even when the office door was tightly shut. Taping was interrupted in various ways – by lawnmowers on the grounds outside the office, by an inmate washing the office window with a squeegee, by nurses looking for inmates, by security doors banging, and by inmates shouting at one another. On one occasion, an interview ended abruptly when I was called upon to help in an emergency situation. A nurse had been sitting with an inmate in an adjacent room when the woman began to relive a rape. The nurse called for help and I intervened, calming the woman, then advising the nurse about further procedures. I returned to the interviewee after about fifteen minutes. She'd been waiting patiently, but with worry for the woman who'd experienced the flashback. We both felt unsettled, acknowledged that fact, and postponed the interview until another day.

The women were separated from their families and friends and were often deeply affected both by what went on 'outside,' at home, and by their powerlessness to affect those events. When one participant, Danielle, arrived at my office in a state of emotional crisis over something that had happened to her daughter, we postponed the taping for a week and used the scheduled interview time for supportive therapy.

At our first meeting, Doris announced that she didn't want to participate after all. When I probed for her reasons, she said, 'I'm not ready for this yet.' I continued to encourage her to sit and talk anyway, and she launched enthusiastically into the details of her life. I interrupted her to say that what she was telling me was exactly the kind of thing we'd be discussing in a formal interview. Her response was 'I know, but I'm just not ready for this. Maybe sometime later, in a month or two.' Having noticed her glance towards the tape recorder when she first arrived, I asked if it was the interview or the tape recorder that concerned her. She replied that the tape recorder didn't 'feel private.' I then offered to take notes in lieu of taping, and she agreed immediately to go ahead on that basis. When, after an hour or more, I announced the end of the interview, she eagerly agreed to set another appointment time for the second interview, exclaiming, 'I still have my life story to tell you!'

THE PARADOX OF OBJECTIVITY

The value of bringing people together and having them talk is undermined if we listen through a filter of prejudice or if we strip their words of their intended meaning. If we are to uncover real knowledge of women in conflict with the law, we must cut through both the irrelevant templates constructed by experts and the prejudices held by society. Attitudes and approaches to research are critical factors in producing research that is valid and useful. There is a tradition in the social sciences of emulating the methods of natural science. In practice, this has produced an uncomfortable union between notions of rigour adopted from the natural sciences and the complex and highly contextual nature of the subjects under investigation in the social sciences. One fundamental principle of the natural sciences, objectivity, is particularly problematic.[7] The notion of objectivity implies that observations are independent of the observer, that the observer is somehow removed from her or his historical context and able to make observations that are independent of her or his bias or subjective interpretation. According to this concept, the values, experiences, and intentions of the observer do not influence his or her perceptions of observed behaviour; the observation process – the research – is assumed to be value-neutral.

Some argue, in contrast, that research cannot be value-neutral, that it is in fact value-bound.[8] Indeed, 'objectivity' carries a value of its own. That value is reflected in the fact that the absence of objectivity is considered to be synonymous with 'researcher bias' and in the assumption that objectivity is desirable. As Hunt explains, 'the personal intentions of researchers, which are the driving force behind the inquiry, are assumed to be negative forces which need to be controlled or eliminated.'[9] Thus, the fear of researcher bias has driven psychologists and other social scientists to deny the existence of their personal intentions and value systems.

Paradoxically, researchers can move towards objectivity only to the extent that they are cognizant of their values, experiences, and intentions. Research can be value-neutral only to the extent that researchers are able to divest themselves of experience and context. Since the latter is practically impossible, research is invariably influenced by the values and intentions of the researcher, the method employed, the assumptions underlying the researcher's theories, and the context in which the research is conducted. Jaggar implies that the denial of personal intentions can be dangerous; she uses as her example the view that 'one who claims to be uncommitted on the question of women's oppression in fact demonstrates tremendous anti-feminist bias.'[10] Surely, if it is not possible or even desirable to escape one's experience, values, and intentions, the responsible and ethical alternative is to uncover, reveal, and manage them, for they are the attributes that determine and characterize the researcher's approach.

In his work on the research process, Hunt proposes that the nature of the approach to research has a significant effect on its results. He emphasizes that the researcher's approach, its impact on the participants, and the usefulness of the research are linked in important ways: 'When researchers treat persons as objects, they learn *only* about their physical movement as physical objects. When researchers treat persons as organisms, they learn *only* about their basic needs and their reflexes. However, when researchers treat those whom they research as persons, then they are more likely to uncover understandings which are relevant to the human condition and therefore contain practical value.'[11] For research subjects to be treated as persons, it is necessary that their words be heard. This is not as straightforward as it may seem, since the perceptions and theories that researchers bring to the research process create a filter through which hearing takes place.

WOMEN'S EXPERIENCES THROUGH WOMEN'S EYES

Wine[12] and Sherif[13] charge that the rhetoric of objectivity has concealed the fact that, until recently, most research has been male-centred. Men have been the researchers, and men have been the subjects of research. Often, male-centred work has been the only research available in a particular field of study, and, consequently, has been applied to women as well as to men. Women's experiences have been interpreted through a masculine filter, which has been concealed by the rhetoric of objectivity.

Interpretation is an important aspect of the research process,[14] and researchers' interpretations are always a product of their own experiences.[15] We each have the capacity to interpret ourselves and our relationships and the outside world, and we do so constantly. We are 'in context,' and we make meaning of our context and ourselves. It is at this point that my theoretical approach intersects with my research approach, for I believe that we cannot know what moves and motivates other persons unless we can understand how they make sense of their worlds.

The critique that has typified feminist work in criminology, as well as feminist research into women's position in the social structure, has produced a foundation for understanding the social structural issues involved in women's lawbreaking. There is also new work in which women's psychological development is being explored. This compelling work has meaning for me, and shaped the lens through which I interpreted the women's stories. In the following paragraphs, I describe the work in psychological development that guided my approach, and in Chapter 2, I discuss the feminist critique of criminology. My understanding of women's position in the social structure is woven throughout.

WOMEN'S DEVELOPMENT IN RELATION

Through studies of the ways in which females and males arrive at moral decisions, Gilligan found important evidence for a mode of women's development that contradicts existing theories in which separation is the goal of psychological development. Gilligan said that she noticed the emergence of different themes that she linked by empirical observation to her research participants by gender. She found that the males she studied tended to base their decisions on a concern with rights and an adherence to rules and regulations, whereas the females were focused on caring and were concerned with conflicting responsibilities. From the females, Gilligan heard evidence of a more relational approach to psychological development.[16]

During the same period, members of the Stone Center group, including Jean Baker Miller, Judith Jordan, Janet Surrey, Alexandra Kaplan, Irene Stiver, and their colleagues, were formulating a theory of women's psychological development based on their work with women.[17] This theory represents an important restructuring in thinking about women's psychological development, emphasizing relationship rather than separation as the vehicle of development. The group has found that mutually empowering relationships, or relationships that are mutually growth-fostering, are both the medium through which development occurs and the goal of development. Their work has involved a reconceptualization of women's development as a function of the capacity for relationships and competence within relationships, and they believe that a growing capacity for empathy is the central organizing feature of women's development. The capacity for empathy begins with the early mother–daughter relationship and develops through practice in relationships. Optimally, it is a mutual process in which all participants experience 'zest or vitality, empowerment to act, knowledge of self and other, self-worth, and the desire for more connection.'[18]

According to this theory, as a woman develops psychologically, she becomes increasingly tolerant of ambiguity, flexible in her interactions with others, and able to respond to contingencies. At the same time, it is her tolerance, flexibility, and responsiveness that are vehicles of her development. A woman's response to another's relational needs is coupled with her attempt to meet her own needs through the relational situation. As her ability to respond to another increases, so does her capacity to participate in growth-enhancing relationships. In a relationship that fosters optimum development, the woman will both give and receive empathic responses. Given the importance of mutuality to the process of development, it follows that 'women are particularly vulnerable to the threat of abandonment, isolation and disconnection,'[19] although Miller argues that women can learn from small disconnections if they are balanced by growth-enhancing connections.[20]

In traditional theories in which the goal of psychological development is separation and autonomy, women's need for attachment and affiliation has been deemed psychopathology. In contrast, the Stone Center group has recognized the value of relational aspects of human existence, such as ongoing connection and the continuing importance of mutually caring relationships, thereby reconceptualizing as healthy development that which has been considered women's psychopathology by traditional, primarily male, theorists.

This theory of relational development is an incomplete and evolving theory – one that is, decidedly, 'in progress.' Like any theory, it is limited by the perspectives of those who have conceived and developed it. The Stone Center group is composed of White, heterosexual, and privileged professional women whose research has focused primarily on White, heterosexual college women. They began their work by examining their own experiences, processes, and perspectives. Recognizing the limitations inherent in their homogeneity, they moved on to 'enlarge' their vision of women's development by hearing the perspectives of women from other 'cultural, political, spiritual, or racial backgrounds.'[21]

By cautiously applying what has been constructed of this new theory of women's development to specific women's stories, we can begin to understand women's lives in a new way, through a lens that is inherently 'of women' rather than 'of men.' In the process, the theory itself is expanded through the incorporation of new information.

IS IT TRUE WHAT WE HEAR?

Through my interviews with the fourteen women whose stories I present in this book, I gathered a volume and quality of material that could have been obtained only within the safe limits of meaningful connections. The research process engendered trust, enabling the women to be candid and forthcoming. In the final interview, I asked the women directly about their experience of the interview process, and their responses confirmed that a valuable connection had indeed been made. They expressed feelings of safety and trust, and comfort with the unregimented style of the interviews. They also said that they did not feel obligated to answer the questions in a particular way, or that I was looking for specific answers. One woman commented on the style of the interviews, saying that if my questioning had been too regimented, I would never have gotten to know her. Similarly, she felt that a questionnaire would not have been effective. She had completed questionnaires in the past, and had often left blank spaces in response to questions that she did not want to answer, or had not answered truthfully.

No attempt was made to 'verify' the women's accounts through file studies[22] or interviews with other people. Indeed, this kind of 'verification' would have contradicted the principles of research that guided the study. None the less, relying on people's subjective accounts can be a challenging experience for all those who have learned to disbelieve. It is at this point that research involving limited numbers of participants meets research that relies on numbers, for there is some reassurance in repetition. While I was interning in the prison, I counselled dozens of women in addition to carrying out the research interviews. I was also exposed to the women in the course of everyday life in the prison. Although no two stories are ever exactly alike, the thoughts, feelings, and issues expressed by the many other women whose stories I heard were similar to those presented here. Numbers aside, there are other ways of confirming the trustworthiness of research, and these are described in Appendix B.

NO SMALL RETURN

In talking to the fourteen women, my goal was to learn from them through a process that would allow all of us to expand our capacity to grow. As hoped, many women felt they had learned something about themselves during the process of the interviews. One said, 'I've learned I'm not a useless person,' while another said, 'Being here has helped more than I thought it would. A lot of times that we've talked it's been very painful, but it's opened a door – it's opened a space to find some positive things, so I'm glad I had the chance to talk.' Another woman said she found out how much anger she felt. Some women found it hard to be interviewed, and one was embarrassed at first to reveal private information. One said, in the last interview, that she still got 'butterflies' whenever she came to talk, because she was not sure if she should continue to 'open up.' Only two women said they were not sure if or how the interviews had helped them. Overall, the women found the experience helpful, sometimes to a much greater degree than they had expected. One woman, who had experienced very little positive human contact in her life, said, 'At least you're sitting and listening to me.'

2

From Separation to Connection

One of our social structures, the judicial system, separates people into groups, the 'inside' and the 'outside,' the 'good' and the 'bad,' the victims and the criminals. The physical separation of people through imprisonment is one way in which we define who we are in the social sphere. The segment of society comprising people who have not been incarcerated tends to exclude people who have been incarcerated.

Separation is not without its advantages. Our whole system of learning is based on separation, which has been pragmatic if not always useful for full understanding; it is easier to manage separate disciplines than to deal with a web of psychological, social, historical, environmental, and political factors.

In the natural sciences, techniques of separation are used to isolate materials from their habitats, in order to facilitate the study of their unique properties. Psychologists, eager to have their work accepted as 'legitimate' science, modelled their own experimental procedures for studying human behaviour on those used in the natural sciences.[1] Hence, psychologists tend to develop theories about individual behaviour without regard to the environment in which the individual exists, thereby implying that people exist in isolation from one another and from society. Similarly, sociologists separate social structures from the thoughts and emotions of individuals.

The women I interviewed showed me the inadequacy of a dichotomous approach to understanding the study of lawbreaking. They identified inimical systems, abusive partners, socioeconomic disadvantage, and difficulties in relationships, but they also believed that they were responsible for their own actions, making statements such as 'No one made me do it.' Judging from their attempts to include external issues along with a recognition of internal processes in their accounts of their conflicts with the law, the women seemed to know implicitly that individuals exist in the context of social structures and that, if their lawbreaking is to be understood, psychological and sociological issues must be taken into account.

From perspectives shaped by separation, we make judgments about ourselves and other people. One of the judgments often made about people who are incarcerated is that they are 'different.' Of course, people are not all alike, and, indeed, most of us like to feel that we're different from other people. We want to feel that we are special in our differentness and that we are accepted despite or perhaps because of it. People who have come into conflict with the law and who have been separated from other people by imprisonment, however, are often considered different in the sense of being anomalous, abnormal, to be feared, and to be ostracized from society. Yet, when I think of the fourteen women I interviewed and the dozens of women I counselled in the prison, I am struck by the basic similarities of their hopes, pain, and dreams to my own and to those of other women who have never been incarcerated – hopes for themselves and their children, the pain of past and present struggles, and dreams of a better life.

FEMALE LAWBREAKERS IN THE LITERATURE

In prominent theories and studies of lawbreaking and criminality, women in conflict with the law have once again been at a disadvantage, on two counts: They have usually been either ignored or added on to studies that focus on men.[2] Merton ignored women in his strain theory,[3] as did Becker in developing his labelling theory.[4] In their theory of differential association, Sutherland and Cressey treated women as adjuncts. They looked at the difference in crime rates between men and women and attributed women's lower rates to factors such as the closer supervision girls tend to receive; the greater emphasis normally placed, with girls, on being 'nice'; and the greater care normally taken in teaching anticriminal behaviour to girls.[5] Hirschi's control theory is essentially a study of conformity. Inexplicably, he analyses only the responses of the males in his sample, even though – if lower crime rates are any indication – women are more conforming than men.[6]

Despite social scientists' concern about 'researcher bias,' they have not traditionally applied that criticism to research that is conducted from an inherently masculine perspective on a male population, and then generalized to a female population. Indeed, this sort of generalization has typified research in the social sciences, including criminology. To compound the problem, when women have been studied, the research has been based on hypotheses rooted in mythical and stereotypical notions of women's 'nature.'

Not surprisingly, the results obtained from such research and theory development have not only impeded understanding, but also fostered spurious 'understandings' of women. Consider the following theories, developed during the past century to explain women's lawbreaking: At the turn of the century, Lombroso and Ferrero took cranial measurements and counted their subjects' moles in an attempt to prove that female criminals could be distinguished from noncriminal women physiologically. These men also believed that female criminals lacked maternal instinct and were therefore more like men than like women.[7] A product of the same era, Freud believed that girls failed to resolve the Oedipus complex because they did not experience castration anxiety, with the result that their superegos were not fully formed.[8] In a curious twist of Freud's theory, Abrahamsen postulated that women became kleptomaniacs because they were unable to achieve sexual gratification as a result of their penis envy and castration anxiety.[9] Psychoanalytically oriented theorists have focused on prostitution and produced a variety of theories – that prostitutes are denying their homosexuality or that they are oversexed, frigid, or acting out hostility towards men through their work. Thomas felt that women's biological makeup influenced their ability to live up to social expectations and that morality was a code of the adult male world, of which women had no experience. In a concession to social influences, he did admit that living up to social expectations was most easily accomplished in the context of economic security.[10] After studying the cases of five hundred women who had been imprisoned, the Gluecks said that the women were 'dealing with a complicated network of biologic and socio-economic deficiencies' but went on to locate the women's criminality in personality variables, calling them a 'sorry lot' who were 'burdened with feeble-mindedness, psychopathic personality, and marked emotional instability.'[11] Role theory, in which Parsons postulated that girls were socialized to be passive, nonviolent, and nurturing, was an attempt to explain why women committed fewer crimes than men.[12] Pollak argued that women had an inherently deceitful nature and committed many more crimes than were reported, but that their physical and psychological constitution enabled them to conceal most of their crimes. He also believed that 'chivalrous' police failed to report many of the crimes committed by women.[13] Konopka perceived her subjects and their lawbreaking quite differently, emphasizing their need for love, protection, and dependency.[14] Cowie, Cowie, and

Slater believed that social and environmental factors were the most important determinants of criminality.[15] These researchers viewed the stresses of the home and the overburdened lives of mothers as the critical factors, and recommended voluntary sterilization and the removal of children from the home when mothers couldn't cope. They also believed that 'genetical factors' played a part in the type of crime committed, and they tried to find a link between multiple Y-chromosomes and crime.[16] Dalton implicated menstruation in criminality;[17] for the past century, researchers have been blaming women's liberation;[18] and Simon suggested that increased opportunities for women contributed to women's criminality.[19]

None of these theories has contributed to a true understanding of women's lawbreaking in all its complexity or to an understanding that might lead to some resolution of the problems involved. If the theories could be seen as part of an unfolding of understanding, one could say that they were historically necessary but obsolete stages of epistemological development. However, remnants of many of the theories continue to inform both popular and professional thought, manifesting themselves in such unproven, and mutually contradictory, beliefs about female lawbreakers as the following: they look different from 'normal' women; they have no conscience; they have no morals; they are cunning and deceitful; they are more like men than like women; they are naturally passive and dependent; they are very smart; they are very dull; they should be kept at home; they are antisocial; the justice system is too easy on them. The contemporary coexistence of such diverse and contradictory theories, along with their stereotypical nature, suggests that the theories have contributed little to our understanding of women who come into conflict with the law. In practice, they may actually interfere with the process of getting to know who these women really are.

Feminist criminologists have emerged as a ray of hope in this field in which women have been so poorly represented. They have worked to alert researchers and theorists to the fact that female lawbreakers are among the least visible and least understood of the larger population of women. Their earliest and still most consequential work is their extensive critique of existing theories of criminality, beginning with Heidensohn's identification of the problem in the late 1960s and her call for a thorough exploration of women's criminality.[20] Klein followed, with her observation that the emphasis in studies of female criminals had been on individual physiological or psychological characteristics to the near exclusion of economic, social, and political factors. According to Klein, the literature on the subject was moralistic and laden with assumptions about women that were disguised as science: the authors of the theories dichotomized the population of women into good, noncriminal women and bad, criminal women.[21]

Hoffman-Bustamente agreed with Klein's assessment,[22] and also resurrected Parsons' role theory[23] as a possible explanation for women's lesser propensity for criminal activity. A first attempt to analyse women's criminality in terms of social relationships, role theory is based on the premise that girls are socialized to be passive, nonviolent, and nurturing, whereas boys are given freedom, allowed to be somewhat aggressive, and encouraged to be ambitious, in the expectation that they will someday support a family financially. Although it was lauded for its promise in explaining differential crime rates for women and men, the theory was limited in its usefulness because it was not helpful in explaining the reasons for women's lawbreaking.

Smart suggested that role-frustration, a variation of role theory, might explain women's criminal behaviour. She hypothesized that women turned to crime because they were frustrated with their limiting sex roles, but she then criticized her own theory on the grounds that it implied psychological and emotional causes.[24] Smart's outright dismissal of psychological implications was unfortunate because it amounted to a denial of women as *both* psychological and social beings. Nevertheless, the trend in the feminist approach to women's lawbreaking has been to discard psychological explanations and to focus on sociological issues.

If there is any explanatory value in the notion of role frustration, it must be applicable to both sex roles. If women's sex role is considered limiting – and therefore frustrating – compared with men's, men's role must be considered more expansive and freeing, and therefore *not* frustrating. Yet men commit crimes in far greater numbers than women. The extant crime rates would suggest that, contrary to the theory, expansive sex roles foster lawbreaking. Alternatively, it may be that men's role is in some way more limiting than women's.

Smart's discussion of role theory appeared in her book *Women, Crime, and Criminology: A Feminist Critique*, which is considered one of the most complete and intellectually rigorous of the feminist critiques.[25] In it, she described the nature of women's criminality and provided detailed criticisms of the work of classic and contemporary theorists of women's criminality, and of their approaches to prostitution, rape, and mental illness. In this pioneering undertaking, Smart examined the treatment of women offenders in Britain's prisons, calling into question the practices of the British judicial system. She linked the basic failings of existing studies of women's criminality to a poor understanding of women, a reliance on a biological model of female behaviour, and an unquestioning acceptance of sexual stereotypes of women and girls. It was her contention that the study of women and criminality – of women as both victims *and* agents of crime – had been neglected. Almost two decades later, the balance has shifted. The notion of women as victims has become a popular subject for research and applied programs; indeed, the concept has become an integral part of feminist theorizing about women's criminality. However, women as agents of lawbreaking have generated nothing that even approaches the same level of professional or public interest.

No sooner had feminists begun their work than a new twist on an old theory appeared, redirecting the course of feminist thinking and truncating feminists' efforts to develop radical approaches to theory in the field.[26] Following in the direction of Pike, Bishop, and Pollak,[27] Adler claimed that she had found a correlation between increases in the arrests of women and the liberation of women.[28] Moving away from biological explanations of gender differences in crime, she postulated that, with the advent of the women's movement, a new female criminal was breaking with her sex role and increasingly turning to crime. Adler credited the women's movement with the power to alter women's self-images, and, like some of her predecessors, she believed that criminal women were more like men than like women. According to Adler, women were moving into new and more serious areas of crime.

At the same time, Simon noticed the increases in arrest rates but realized that arrests had increased for property crimes, such as fraud, larceny, and embezzlement, but not for violent crimes.[29] She suggested that increased opportunities for women were a factor contributing to the increases. Whereas many women previously had remained in the home, where they had few opportunities to break the law, they were now suddenly out in the workplace, where they found many such opportunities. Worrall, by contrast, believed that such reasoning obscured important findings: 'Valuable insights into the poverty and oppression which correlate with much female crime have been confounded by assertions that liberation from traditional social constraints will inevitably result in more crimes of affluence and violence among women.'[30]

The idea of hypothesizing a similar link for men – that increased opportunities in the workplace for men lead to crime – seems absurd. When men's lawbreaking has been studied in relation to employment, the hypothesis has typically been formed from the opposite end of the opportunity continuum – that is, that *less* opportunity, or unemployment, leads to crime.

None the less, Adler and Simon redirected the attention of feminists and provoked ardent rebuttals for more than a decade. The two authors' methods were criticized[31] and their theoretical premises attacked.[32] Some researchers attempted empirical studies to test their claims, with variable results.[33] Chesney-Lind defended the women's movement,[34] as did James and Thornton, who studied the self-reports of 287 girls and found that those who were feminist were actually less likely to break the law than those who were more traditional.[35] Even a failure of the women's movement – that it did not result in greater employment opportunities for lower-class women, who were the most likely to be incarcerated – was used to buttress the defence.[36]

Smart understood that to blame the women's movement for changes in the behaviour of women was to oversimplify the issue. She argued that the effects of the women's movement could be understood only within the context of history and of the political and economic circumstances of the era.[37] Naffine cautioned that Smart pursued her point too far, however, negating the impact of women's activism on the social structure.[38] In effect, Smart did the very thing that she had criticized: she overlooked the role of women's agency, or women's instrumentality, in criminality. In my interviews with the fourteen women for the present study, it became clear that the issue of instrumentality was fundamental to understanding the women's conflicts with the law.

Perhaps as a result of the backlash against Adler's and Simon's claims, there has been relatively little movement in research looking at female lawbreakers as agents, despite the need for it. Instead, feminists have concentrated on women as victims of crime and poverty, on methodological approaches, on debates about issues such as the adequacy of role theory in explanations of women's lawbreaking, and on the women's liberation hypotheses. The nature of feminist involvement in criminology and the appropriateness of developing a separate criminology of women have also been debated.[39] These arguments have been a feature of discussion since Smart first worried that male criminologists might co-opt this 'new' area of study or that a separate criminology might marginalize women.[40] The latter, at least, is a hollow concern if feminists' only concerns are for the lawbreakers, because female lawbreakers are already marginalized in the sense that they are barely visible to the criminologists whom feminists view as 'mainstream.'[41] Moreover, the concern seems groundless when one considers the gaps that would still exist in our understanding of women's position in society if Chesler had never focused exclusively on women in psychiatric hospitals[42] or if Brownmiller had never studied women and rape.[43]

Research efforts by feminists have been characterized by analyses of the social structure[44] and have been focused on White women.[45] In attempting to understand the sociopolitical roots of women's criminality, feminists have focused on women's poverty, an approach well rooted in the past. Windschuttle posited that the idea, popular with socialists in the mid-1800s, was politically motivated. It was promoted 'by social reformers who wanted to clean up pockets of poverty, and feminists wanting legal rights and opportunities expanded for women.'[46] The social-reform focus on poverty as the cause of women's crime was sustained through the nineteenth century, then punctuated by more 'scientific' explanations, which implicated the individual, in the early and mid twentieth century. Although it has been resurrected in recent years, the assumption that poverty can explain all or most crimes committed by women appears to have no empirical foundation. Nevertheless, the notion of a poor, struggling mother, forced to the streets to feed her children, has tended to drive any compassionate thinking about women and crime.

It is clear from Carlen's discussion of the issue in *Women, Crime, and Poverty*[47] that she understood that there was no clear statistical link between lawbreaking and poverty. In carrying out her ethnographic study of the criminal careers of thirty-nine women in Britain, she attempted to honour the uniqueness of each woman's story, and she included rich, descriptive material in her outline of the study. In forcing poverty as her thesis, however, she ignored much that might have been of value in her research. The women she interviewed tended not to identify any single cause for their lawbreaking; among the causes they cited most frequently were the following: 'desire for more money, problems associated with being in residential "Care," drug (including alcohol) problems, plus the quest for excitement.'[48] Only twelve of the women identified poverty as the reason for their lawbreaking, and those twelve had 'wildly differing perceptions' of the ways in which it had contributed to their becoming lawbreakers. Yet, instead of taking the women at their word and moving more deeply into their stated reasons and meanings, Carlen focused on the 'objective criteria,' through which she determined that thirty-seven of the thirty-nine women had at some time in their lives experienced poverty. She justified her approach by discrediting her chosen methodology: she cited two standard criticisms of ethnographies, namely, that they can only describe, not explain, and that there are endless numbers of meanings that can be taken from them. She approached her task by 'deconstructing [the women's criminal] careers into the elemental ideological and political components which many of them share, albeit in the different combination that renders each unique.'[49] Although she made the valuable observation that female lawbreakers from lower socioeconomic groups were more likely to be criminalized than middle-class female lawbreakers, she forfeited the opportunity to learn from the women who contributed so much to her research. She also failed to clarify the actual role of poverty in lawbreaking.

Perhaps poverty as a cause of crime is invoked frequently because it seems to make intuitive sense. But one need only compare the data describing women's economic situation and women's crime with the parallel data for men to see that linear causality cannot be assumed. Women own less property, earn less money, and commit fewer crimes; men own more property, earn more money, and commit more crimes. Of course, these statements, too, are generalizations and cannot necessarily be applied to individual situations. The effects of poverty on women and women's reactions to poverty are complex. Overgeneralizations linking poverty and lawbreaking are unfair to women and men living below the poverty line, including single mothers who work hard to support their children and who, with careful management, resourcefulness, and perhaps help from family and friends, live within the constraints of their meagre budgets.

Despite the fact that they discuss women only in terms of their social position, feminist criminologists from several countries have made important contributions to the study of female lawbreakers. (Regrettably, I have been unable to access one source close to home – that is, the body of work produced by francophone feminist criminologists in Canada.) In the English-language work, key issues have been identified, such as the categorization and subordination of women lawbreakers on the basis of their sex, the prevalence of abuse and difficult relationships in their backgrounds, and their resistance to oppression. The work has been valuable because it has added credence to the feminist critique and expanded the base for the development of theory in the future. It has also furnished examples of the ways in which women are victimized, then often revictimized, by the justice system. None the less, feminists working in the area of criminology are leaning towards the notion that a reconceptualization must occur in which women are perceived as agents of their own experience. Mathews approached adolescent prostitution from this perspective, reframing it as a solution or a method of meeting needs when choices have been restricted.[50]

A structural analysis cannot answer all questions, simply because women are neither exclusively social beings nor members of any single race or culture. To ignore the psychological aspects of an entire group is to miss the diversity and depth that lead to understanding. In *Offending Women: Female Lawbreakers and the Criminal Justice System,*[51] Worrall notes the contradiction inherent in a structural analysis in which individual factors are ignored. Worrall suggests that the plight of the individual offender has been overlooked, as has the plight of those who are in a position to help her.

Women are psychological as well as social beings. They are not empty shells, passively accepting oppression and victimization.[52] A feminist analysis that is limited to women's position as victims in the social structure is ultimately no more helpful than an analysis that depicts them as morally 'fallen.' As Widom puts it, 'the most promising explanation of female criminality is likely to be multifaceted and approached from a multidisciplinary perspective encompassing psychological, economic, social, legal and historical factors.'[53]

CONNECTING WITH FEMALE LAWBREAKERS

The women whose stories appear in this book (and others like them) have been rendered invisible when they have not been misunderstood, unfairly treated, or condemned outright. By presenting their stories in a way that accurately reflects their experiences, I hope to convey what it is to be such a woman in this world of masculine perceptions, images, and structures. At the same time, it is not my purpose to minimize the seriousness of the women's actions. My hope is that a move towards greater understanding will lead to new directions in research and dialogue, and to solutions.

To reduce the possibility of distortion in the retelling of the women's stories, I have stayed close to their language and, wherever possible, have avoided using summary terms. To create order while maintaining the integrity of the material, I looked for common themes in the women's stories. I found that the most veridical method was to start by identifying the women's reasons for breaking the law. This approach – starting with the women's own reasons for breaking the law and remaining close to their experiences as they described them – proved to be a constant challenge to constraining ideologies. Paradoxically, it was by staying close to the women's descriptions of their experiences that I was able to assimilate the similarities and differences emerging from their stories and to identify the unifying features.

The differences evident among the stories suggest that there is no universal women's experience. Rather, women's experiences vary with the class, race, and culture to which the women belong, their family relationships, and their own perception of themselves in relation to all these facets of their lives. However, the women also shared many common experiences, not only with one another, but also with women who have never been incarcerated. The similarities with women who have not come into conflict with the law provide strong evidence that the women presented here are not anomalous women who are deviant by nature.

3

The Women's Words: Need

Marianne, Jacqueline, Connie, Arlene, and Rose believe that their law-breaking was a function of need. All of the Black women interviewed (Jacqueline, Arlene, and Rose) explained their conflict with the law in this way. The word *need* was selected from the women's words to capture their stories because it can be used to refer either to material (financial or physical) 'wanting' or to emotional 'wanting.' For the five women who indicated that they broke the law because of need – sometimes a feeling of 'desperate need' – the physical and emotional domains were bound together.

Four of the five women broke the law in order to provide food, medicine, and other necessities of life for their children and themselves. Although these are physical needs, emotional need also figured prominently in each of these women's stories, and it was the most important element of the fifth woman's story.

MARIANNE

Marianne, a forty-two-year-old Caucasian mother of two teenaged children, described herself as a caring but outspoken person. She said that she could not 'let things lie,' and that she was a very angry person.

During her marriage, Marianne felt she could never do anything right, including giving birth (her babies were born prematurely). She felt she received no emotional support from her husband. When the marriage ended, her husband refused to pay support, despite court orders and a well-paying job. Marianne tried to have the court orders enforced but her legal-aid lawyer was no match for her husband's 'hot-shot' lawyer. Worse, her husband told the children that she was trying to take his money and put him in jail. Eventually, she gave up, put all the court orders in a box, sealed it, and never looked at them again. Her husband 'cried to his employer' about the pressure he was experiencing and took a year's leave of absence from work, during which time he was supported by another woman.

Marianne worked as a bookkeeper for a prominent businessman and local politician. She was underpaid: after almost nine years of employment, she was earning only $21,000. She was a 'very dedicated employee' and a good friend to her employer. When he left his wife she was 'there' for him, although he didn't return the favour when *her* marriage ended. When he came under scrutiny for inappropriate billings, she covered for him, saying that she had made a mistake.

When Marianne's marriage ended, she moved with the children from a four-bedroom house into a two-bedroom apartment, but often had trouble paying the rent. On the rare occasion that she bowed to pressure and asked her family for financial assistance, they refused it. When her husband opted out of work, she had no drug coverage, and on one occasion, when her daughter was ill, Marianne was forced to seek help from her church. The minister came to her home and provided the necessary medication as well as emotional support. He later told Marianne that, if she needed help in the future, she should come to him, so that her neighbours would not see them together. He had apparently received a telephone call from a neighbour who was a friend of her husband's. The neighbour made substantial donations to the church.

Marianne's father was a prominent person in her life; she hated him and was terrified of him. The son of an alcoholic mother and product of a horrendous childhood, he was a 'weekend alcoholic' who frequently blackened her mother's eyes. On one occasion, he hit her sister, and Marianne jumped on his back and hit him. He would come home drunk and she would hide in a closet. She remembered driving with him when she was about ten years old; he was drunk, and she had to pull on the steering wheel to avoid an accident. When they got home, she 'got hell' from her mother for 'letting' him get drunk.

Marianne's father died when she was twenty-two. Despite the bad times, her father could be caring; he was the parent who tended her after her appendectomy. Marianne also recalled that he never missed a day of work. In fact, he had a strong work ethic and 'drilled and drilled and drilled' into her head that one didn't depend on the government or anyone else, for any reason. One stood on one's own two feet.

As a teenager, Marianne found comfort in her high school sweetheart, whose parents also drank. When she was eighteen, they became engaged and planned to marry in spite of her father's disapproval. Shortly before the wedding date, her fiancé was killed in a car accident. Around the same time, her father thrust her into the world with five dollars and orders to go to the city, stay with her sister, and not return until she'd found work. She did find work, and she stayed in the city until she married.

After she divorced, Marianne found that she couldn't survive on her salary without financial support from her husband. To make ends meet, she began to 'borrow' money from her employer without asking (she would later replace it). Even so, the financial pressure was too great, and one day she simply went to the home of her husband and his new wife and turned her children over to them. The following day, her husband ended his leave of absence.

The borrow-and-replace cycle continued for five years until she had 'borrowed' $40,000, which she was unable to repay. She became uncomfortable with the situation, antagonized her employer and co-workers, and eventually agreed with her employer that she should leave. She was fully aware that her theft would be discovered once she had left the position, so she went home and waited to be arrested. The crime was Marianne's first offence, and it came as a shock to all who knew her.

CONNIE

Thirty-one-year-old Connie, a Caucasian woman, was the third of four children. Her mother worked as a clerk in a small business and her father had been a construction supervisor. Her father was an alcoholic who, Connie said, had a reason to drink: he had lost a leg in a work-related accident and had been laid off for the first five years of Connie's life. (He 'babysat' Connie during those years.) The drinking had started before that, however, and her mother had left her father before Connie was born, after a fight during which her father had hit her mother. Connie was never able to understand why her mother went back to her father, and she blamed her mother for wrecking the lives of her siblings and herself by doing so. She did not accept her mother's excuse that there was 'no mothers' allowance' then, because her mother had always been employed.

Connie's father drank almost every day. He beat her two older brothers but not her or her younger sister. Her mother would say that she hoped Connie's father would die; sometimes, she would threaten him, saying 'I'll kill you.' Connie worried about fire, knowing that her father wouldn't be able to get out of a burning house without his artificial leg, which he took off every night. She remembered hiding with her mother and siblings outside in the snow, or going for a walk, until her father took off his leg and went to bed. When he took off his leg, he was harmless. Connie felt that she had 'never had a childhood.'

Connie thought her mother despised her because her father raised her when she was young. She was 'attached' to him; he was the one who showed her affection, not her mother.

Although he never beat her, Connie's father lectured her constantly. He 'pumped into our heads that if you want anything, you've got to go and get it because it won't come to you.' Her interpretation of his lectures was that she had to work for whatever she wanted.

When Connie was about twenty-four, her mother left her father, saying she would not return unless he stopped drinking. Connie said that he did stop drinking, but her mother never returned. Her father subsequently committed suicide. Connie blamed her mother, saying that she might as well have shot him herself.

Connie married for the first time at the age of nineteen. She left her husband after six months, because he wouldn't let her get a job or a driver's licence. When they divorced, she received a settlement of $27,000, which she gave to her father to buy a truck. She said she didn't need the money at the time, because she was working at two jobs, her day job in a store and nights in a bar, from 6 P.M. until 2 A.M. When she married the second time, her father returned $13,000 for a deposit on a house.

Connie's second husband was the father of her two children. She felt he was a good father, but when he was laid off work, he became a different person. Their marriage ended when she discovered that he had abused one of the children. The man with whom she lived after her second marriage took one of her boys on a trip that was to have lasted twenty-four hours. When they failed to return, Connie notified police; they were found a week later. Connie's fourth relationship lasted about a year, until the man shot at her one day.

Connie believed that she was 'naive' in her judgment of people and in her personal relationships. One such naive judgment eventually led to her incarceration. She met a woman – 'a really nice person' – at the home of a mutual acquaintance, and they became fast friends. The woman's husband was self-employed, and because Connie had previously worked in the accounting department of a large company, the woman asked her if she would be interested in doing his bookkeeping. Connie accepted the offer of work without having met the man; because she liked the woman, she assumed her husband would be 'OK.'

After she'd worked for the man for about three months, he asked her if, when preparing his income tax return, she would find a way to hide $90,000. She refused at first, until he told her he would find someone else to do it if she wouldn't. Connie didn't want to lose her income and eventually agreed. She maintained that it wasn't the thought of money, but of providing for her children, that motivated her. She charged the man $3500 for the service, and she declared the amount on her income tax return.

A few months later, the man asked her for another favour. When she refused, he accused her of stealing from him. At first, Connie couldn't understand why he would accuse her and risk an investigation into his business, but then she realized that he believed nothing would happen to him because he was well known in the community. 'To the courts, this guy is a good member of society.'

This was not Connie's first or most recent brush with the law. At eighteen, she was caught shoplifting mascara, and when her second marriage ended, she wrote some bad cheques for household items and was ordered to pay restitution (about $300). There were also outstanding charges against her: when she moved back to her home town after her marriage ended, she bore the cost of rent and other expenses, but had no money to pay for utilities, and the weather was cold. Her 'mothers' allowance' cheque was delayed, and she received a replacement cheque from the welfare office. When the original cheque arrived in the mail, she cashed it and paid her bills instead of returning it. Meanwhile, she had gone to various agencies for help and had asked her mother for a loan. The agencies were unable to help and her mother refused, saying she had Christmas presents to buy. Connie felt desperate and lost, and said that if she ever found herself in a situation like that again, she would consider suicide.

ARLENE

Arlene, age twenty-seven, is of mixed race, predominantly Black. Her parents married when her mother was nineteen and pregnant with her, and her father was seventeen. She had three younger sisters who were all employed and who had never been in trouble with the law.

When she was very young, Arlene lived with her parents and sisters in a house they shared with her paternal grandmother. When she was four, they moved to a house where they shared facilities with other roomers. She believes that her father began to abuse her mother during their stay in that house. Her father was 'never around much' and never gave them much attention, but neither did he beat her or her sisters. 'He got his fun out of beating my mother.' Arlene never thought of her father as a bad person for beating her mother, because she was an adult who could take care of herself.

Once, her uncle, who lived in the same house, walked in when her father was beating her mother. A fight took place, and her uncle stabbed her father. Arlene's mother pushed her out of the room and never discussed it with her until Arlene asked about it years later.

When Arlene was about five years old, her mother left her father and took her and her sisters to live with her great grandmother and an aunt. Her father later kidnapped one of her sisters, who was later found living with her paternal grandmother. Arlene and her other sisters soon went to live with that grandmother as well, while her mother stayed behind for two years, working to save money so they could get back together; they visited on weekends.

After Arlene's mother took back her daughters, it fell to Arlene to take responsibility for her younger sisters until her mother got home from work every day at 6 P.M. Although there was only a small age difference between her and her sisters, it seemed to Arlene that she was much more mature.

Her mother remarried when Arlene was fifteen. Arlene didn't like her stepfather because he tried to discipline her 'in his own way' and because he changed some of the rules and understandings she'd had with her mother, which resulted in screaming matches that were mediated by her mother. However, they were better off financially with the stepfather and 'always lived like middle class.'

Arlene said her mother seemed to have a 'dual personality': she was very 'sweet,' but could also argue. She was a good mother and she was religious, and everyone who knew her respected her. Arlene had always felt close to her mother and 'could always tell her anything,' but when she went to her at the age of seventeen and asked her about birth control, her mother yelled at her about keeping her virginity, and talked her out of putting herself on birth control.

Arlene hadn't liked high school; there was a lot of peer pressure to skip classes and smoke marijuana, which she tried but didn't like. She graduated after Grade 12 and went to business school for fifteen months, after which she found work doing word processing.

Born and raised in the United States, Arlene was 'normally a working person.' She had her own apartment and a four-year-old daughter when she became pregnant a second time and was laid off her job. She fell behind in her rent and was feeling desperate for money, so she went to the welfare office, but was told that she was not eligible for assistance because she was not actively looking for work.

Outside the welfare office and in obvious distress, Arlene saw a man she knew as an acquaintance, who asked her what was wrong. She told him about her situation and he said he could help her out. He would pay her, in advance, to take 'a package' to Canada; he knew she'd been to Canada once before and so was familiar with customs procedures.

Arlene spent 'three or four days' considering the man's offer before she agreed to carry the package. She thought that her decision to go through with it may have been motivated by anger, since she had been approached immediately after her ordeal at the welfare office. She did not consider the wrongdoing of carrying the package, or the possible effect the drugs it contained could have on other people's lives. She did think about the money that would enable her to start paying off her bills and get her life back together, and she convinced herself that she wouldn't get caught the first time.

When she reached the airport, she thought for a few minutes, 'What am I doing? What if I get caught?' but she 'cut off' her thoughts and feelings, and went on. Arlene was arrested at the airport in Canada, carrying cocaine in a body pack. She found out later that the drugs had a street value of $65,000.

Arlene's mother had not been aware of the financial problems Arlene was having. When she found out later, she said she would have helped out. But Arlene had always wanted to maintain her independence, even from marriage, so that she could be in control of her own life. Moreover, Arlene had always thought of her mother as someone who needed *her* help. When Arlene was young and her mother was raising her and her younger sisters on her own, there was no extra money. Arlene's sisters were demanding, but she couldn't be that way, and always thought about the price of things before she asked for anything. Since Arlene was the oldest sister, she felt she had to be more mature, but she had always wished she had an older sibling, somebody who could take responsibility.

ROSE

Thirty-year-old Rose is a Black woman and the mother of four children. Rose was raised in a 'good,' 'respectable' family. They lived on a farm and always had enough to eat; although her clothes often came from the Salvation Army and were not stylish, they were always neat and clean. Her parents were very strict, and she rarely had friends visit her home; work came first. Rose felt the main thing her parents had done for her was to give her 'lots of love.' She said her mother was 'always there' for her and would always try to explain things to her.

Rose was the second oldest in her family. A sister died in a car crash at the age of nine. Rose was eleven at the time, and she was also in the car; it was driven by a family friend who was injured in the accident. Rose dragged her sister out of the car but when she saw blood coming from her sister's head and neck, she let her drop. Her sister was lying on the ground, still alive, but Rose didn't do anything; she didn't scream, didn't call anybody, couldn't talk, and just stood, looking and crying. She felt that she had just stood there, wanting her sister to die. Later, a doctor said that if her sister had been brought to the hospital a little earlier, she would have lived. Because she hadn't tried to do anything, Rose felt responsible for her sister's death. At the funeral home, Rose 'jumped into the coffin' with her sister and said, 'I'm going, too. I took your life and now I'll take mine.' Because of the state she was in, Rose wasn't allowed to attend her sister's funeral. After her sister died, Rose was 'torn apart' and was put into the 'crazy house.' Rose connected her sister's death with her inability to get close to other women – she was afraid they would kill her.

Rose's parents and grandparents lived close together, and Rose usually spent alternate weeks living in each home in order to perform chores in both. When her sister died, Rose's grandmother was in the hospital. Rose went to see her three days after the accident, and her grandmother died while she was in the room. Rose wanted to take her own life at that point.

Rose's grandfather died five days later. While the others were at the grandfather's funeral, Rose's oldest brother made up a dummy using the grandfather's clothes, stuck a knife in the area of the heart, poured ketchup on the 'wound,' and showed it to Rose when she returned. Rose fell to the floor screaming. She was returned to the hospital, where she stayed for three months.

This behaviour on the part of Rose's oldest brother was typical of him. When Rose was a child, he had taken her along to break into the house of an old man. Her brother gave her a hammer and told her to hit the man, who was sitting in a chair. She refused.

One day, three years after the three family deaths, Rose was on her way home from school when she saw one cousin push another young cousin into a swimming pool. Rose couldn't swim so she just watched and cried. Her mother told her she could have saved him if she'd tried, and her aunt, the child's mother, blamed her for the death.

As a child, Rose was 'always on the go.' Her mother called her a 'little tramp,' and a 'tomboy,' because she always hung out with boys, never girls. She said girls didn't like her and called her names, although she said she felt closer to some White girls than to the Black girls in her school.

Rose quit school in Grade 10, when she became pregnant. She lived with the father of her children for ten years, and began to work the streets after he left the family, in order to feed her children. She had been working as a prostitute in her home town without arrest for about two years when she decided to move.

In her new location, Rose supported herself and her children with the help of welfare assistance, by working as a housekeeper, and through prostitution. One night, with a woman who was also working as a prostitute, she tried some cocaine out of curiosity. Although she had never used drugs before, cocaine made her feel good, and she immediately wanted more. She said that because of her very serious habit – freebasing cocaine – she was eventually cut off welfare. As her habit worsened, Rose neglected her children and herself. She gained and lost weight, swinging as much as fifty pounds in one direction or the other. Her drug habit was particularly hard to break because she was well known as a drug user, and all her friends were drug users. Without drugs, she had no friends.

Rose said she had never been arrested until she started using drugs. Her drug use made her 'careless,' and she began to find prostitution dangerous, not because she was threatened by her 'dates,' but because she was unable to sense when the driver of a car she got into might be an undercover cop. She eventually accumulated several charges relating to prostitution, resisting arrest, and missing court appearances.

JACQUELINE

Jacqueline arrived in Canada with her family twenty-one years before she and I met, at the age of about twelve. She was the oldest child and had three half-sisters. The two youngest girls were the daughters of the man Jacqueline called 'father,' a White businessman who adopted her when he married her mother. The second-oldest sister, Beth, four years younger than Jacqueline, had a different white father. Jacqueline was the only sister who had a Black father. She looked different from the rest of the family; the other three sisters could pass as full sisters. Her family called her the 'black sheep,' and when her parents talked about 'the girls,' Jacqueline felt that they were not including her.

Jacqueline knew nothing about her biological father apart from the fact that he was Black, still living, and about six feet two inches tall. Her mother never told her about her father; in fact, she beat her once for asking about him. In response to Jacqueline's questions, her mother would say, 'He never did anything for you. Why do you want to know?' Jacqueline thought the man might even be unaware of her existence.

When she was very young, Jacqueline lived with an aunt and her grandmother, whom she considered her parents. Her mother was always away 'travelling abroad' and would show up 'once in a while,' so, as a child, Jacqueline did not know her. When Beth was born, they all went to live with Beth's father. He left them after two or three years.

One summer, when she was about six or seven, she was sent to stay with a friend of her mother's, and the woman's common-law husband. The woman left for work early in the morning, and Jacqueline was left in the man's care. On two of those early mornings, he 'raped' her. Jacqueline wasn't sure if there was penetration but remembers thinking she'd 'peed' herself. She never told anyone. Although she wasn't sure what was going on, she knew it wasn't right. After the incidents, Jacqueline got up every morning with the woman and insisted on accompanying her to her workplace.

When Jacqueline went to live with her mother and her new husband, she became the 'family maid.' In her life with her grandmother and aunt, things had been done for her, but suddenly she became the person who took care of others. When the family moved to Canada, the situation became even worse. Both parents went to work full time, and Jacqueline was given full responsibility for her younger sisters, who played while she carried out the household duties on her own. She'd get them ready for school in the morning, come home from school to give them lunch, and watch them while she prepared dinner after school. If her sisters 'took off' and her mother found out, Jacqueline got 'slapped around.' She finally started to punish her sisters, 'beating the daylights out of them,' or locking them in her mother's room, rather than have them take off.

Jacqueline always felt she was 'on the outside looking in' when her sisters received things. When her sister had trouble in math, her father hired a tutor; when Jacqueline had problems with school work, she got 'a slap in the face' and was told to 'do better.' She tried to make herself invisible because she 'never really felt a part of everything.'

Because of her duties at home, Jacqueline couldn't join in the activities at school. To make matters worse, she was sent to a high school where there were hardly any Blacks; she felt very uncomfortable there.

Jacqueline left home at nineteen, in Grade 12, after an incident at the family dinner table. A sister had her elbows on the table and the father scolded her; when she didn't listen, he threw a knife at her. Jacqueline protested, and the scene escalated, with her father grabbing Jacqueline around the neck and choking her. When she didn't relent, her mother piped in, 'She's swearing. Hit her. Why is she talking to you like that?' Jacqueline overturned the dining table, escaped her father's grasp, grabbed a few belongings and her bank book, and left. She returned only to get the rest of her things. Her parents gave her no financial support after she left home.

Jacqueline found a room in a rooming house almost immediately, but ran first to the home of the boyfriend she would eventually marry. He was one of her few friends – 'women, girlfriends, come very far and few between' – and their friendship led to an unsuccessful marriage.

Jacqueline considered herself a principled person who was more concerned for other people than for herself. She always tried to make up for the shortcomings of her biological father so that her mother would look up to her. She always felt she had to prove to her family that she could 'make it' on her own. She wanted to show her family that she didn't need them and that she was as good as her sisters.

Jacqueline believed that she was an 'emotional offender,' because she was driven to what she did mostly by emotions rather than by physical need. She didn't know whom she was offending, herself or somebody else, because she felt she did more harm to herself than to anyone else. Jacqueline had worked in the accounting department of a large company, and stole $42,000 from her employer by writing cheques to herself. Ten years earlier, she had taken $2000 from her former employer, for which she paid full restitution. On both occasions, she took the money to set herself up in a new apartment. In the more recent case, she also gave money to friends and family, bought gifts for her family, and took a vacation 'back home,' taking gifts of money for her relatives. Jacqueline said that she was 'not an upfront thief': she would never shoplift or write a bad cheque because she didn't want to 'tarnish' her credit rating.

DECIPHERING 'NEED'

Expectations versus Limitations

For all five women, a sense of desperation arose from their need to maintain their homes and to continue to provide for their children and/or themselves. The needs they experienced included the need to live up to the expectations of their families.

All the women came from families of origin in which one or both parents were employed. None spoke of material deprivation as children; Rose's clothes did come from the Salvation Army but food was plentiful, because her family lived on a farm. Arlene said her family had always 'lived like middle class,' a comment that contradicts the description she gave of the neighbourhood in which she lived with her mother and two sisters before her mother remarried. She said the children played in the streets and two sisters had been hit by cars, which was not an unusual occurrence in the neighbourhood. Moreover, before her parents' separation, the family had lived in a boarding house. None the less, at other times in her life, the family situation was somewhat better, and Arlene's overall recollection was that she was not materially deprived.

In adulthood, four of the five women were always employed, if not steadily, then at least seasonally. There were other women in the study who, from an outsider's perspective, would be considered to have been in greater need, in the sense of not having a stable home or adequate nourishment, than at least four of the five women who explained their actions as arising out of need. Yet the sense of need among the latter was clearly real, sometimes to the point of desperation. Their situations were complex, reflecting not only financial issues but also the pressures they felt in living up to certain expectations that they had internalized. For example, all the women felt a strong sense of independence; they felt they had to manage entirely on their own. Moreover, their sense of being alone in their struggles was reinforced by their experiences with both family members and social agencies.

For both Marianne and Connie, a strong sense of independence emerged from families in which the work ethic was emphasized fervently. Marianne's father cautioned against support from government or anyone else. With his words ringing in her ears, Marianne was unable to consider welfare or other forms of assistance. Connie's father 'pumped' into her head that anything she wanted she had to 'go and get,' because it would not come to her. He taught her to rely solely on herself, and, although she did receive unemployment insurance or welfare assistance from time to time, she worked whenever she could.

For Arlene, the emphasis on independence came from her mother, who had supported her family by working concurrently at two jobs. Arlene did not want to ask her mother for money for several reasons. She knew that if she did ask, she would be given the inevitable lecture about saving 'for a rainy day.' But her reluctance also stemmed from her childhood, when her mother was raising her and her sisters alone. In those days, Arlene had learned to be undemanding despite the fact that her younger sisters did not hesitate to make their wishes known. Arlene wanted her family to see her as a good and responsible person.

Arlene remained single because she didn't want to relinquish her independence. When she became pregnant a second time, she did not tell the father. She did not solicit his support, financial or other, preferring to avoid dependence on anybody.

Rose was told in an indirect but apparently effective way that she should manage without help. When she was very young, she went to live with her grandparents for the purpose of working for them. When her mother requested that she return home, it was because the mother needed help. A period of indecision ensued, resulting in the division of Rose's time between her grandparents and parents, alternating weeks between homes until her grandparents died. In effect, she was given the responsibility of caring for two generations of her family.

Although Jacqueline used the money that she stole from her employer to purchase tangible items, she believed that her real motivation was emotional rather than physical need. She said that 'half of what happened' to her happened because her parents 'pushed' her 'all the time.' She claimed that her mother was a very materialistic person who expected to be given gifts frequently. Jacqueline said that whenever she purchased something for herself, her mother would complain that she hadn't bought anything for her. In addition, Jacqueline always felt that she needed to compensate for the putative shortcomings of her biological father, and the gifts that she gave her mother were one way of doing so. The situation was exacerbated for Jacqueline by her parents' frequent comments to the effect that 'You're never going to make it. You're always going to be dependent on this one or that one.'

Although there is nothing inherently wrong with being encouraged to fend for oneself, for these women the social values transmitted through the family were on a collision course with the limitations imposed on women in this society, as well as with their own minimal qualifications for employment. The social values transmitted through the family are rarely based on an understanding of the real limitations that are imposed on women as they attempt to earn a living. Moreover, as in the case of these five women, the messages transmitted to women are often contradictory. Women are expected to be passive and dependent but to manage without assistance if they are not in a relationship with a man.

The five women discussed in this chapter learned early in life that they were expected to be independent. Most were the sole providers of the physical, emotional, financial, and safety needs of their children. Of course, the women were also responsible for their own survival and maintenance. However, family members who stressed independence (usually the fathers) had no apparent appreciation of the requirements of the task, of the obstacles the women faced, or of the fact that women have substantially less earning power than men. Although society has always systemically and overtly supported higher wages for men in recognition of their financial responsibility to their families, no such concession has ever been granted to women who support their families. Even Arlene's mother, who was single herself during Arlene's school years, seemed unsympathetic. Perhaps she had forgotten that, when she was a single parent, she had been assisted by relatives. Similarly, Arlene overlooked the differences between her own situation and that of her mother and, instead of asking for help, berated herself for spending all the money she had earned rather than saving it, as her mother had always done.

The women had internalized the expectations of their families and were determined to adhere to them, even though they all faced very difficult circumstances. The four women with children were solely responsible for their children's financial maintenance. Marianne, Connie, and Arlene felt some pressure – and desire – to provide their children with material items so their children could appear to be keeping up with the lifestyles of their friends, while Rose's concern was simply to keep her children fed and attending school. Rose had received only sporadic support for her children when their father was sober and drug-free, but that support disappeared completely when he left the family. Connie was forced to raise her children on her own after separating from her husband, who had abused one of the children, and Arlene had neither requested nor received support from the father of her daughter, even after losing her job. Marianne was especially bitter about her ex-husband's ability to avoid support payments. His nonsupport ultimately resulted in her turning over the children to him and his new wife, a turn of events that she had long fought to avoid.

For Jacqueline, the issue of measuring up to family expectations had strong emotional overtones. She never felt 'good enough' to be considered part of the family; certainly, she felt that she was inadequate in comparison with her sisters, and she was aware that her parents treated them differently. It was her belief that her Black biological father might have been a factor in her differential treatment by her stepfather. Jacqueline's appearance was noticeably different from that of her half-sisters.

In reaction to her feelings that she didn't belong in the family, Jacqueline made a point of demonstrating to her family that she did not need to depend on them. She bought things for her family to prove that she was their equal and should be accepted by them. Like many people, she and her family believed what our society tells us to believe: that our value and right to belong are contingent on our colour and on what we can buy.

The women's earning power was constrained both by the limitations that are placed on women's salaries in our society and by their own, relatively low, levels of education. Although these five women were among the best educated of the women I interviewed, only Arlene had any postsecondary training. Connie and Jacqueline had completed Grade 12. Marianne had completed only Grade 11; she felt that she could not compete for jobs that required skills such as word processing, but didn't have the money or the time to upgrade. Rose had completed Grade 10. With the exception of Rose, all the women worked at clerical jobs that are typically poorly paid and often the first to be eliminated when work slowdowns occur. Rose worked at housekeeping jobs, which are classified as unskilled labour.

The women's choices were also limited – or, perhaps, determined – by their obligations. Connie had usually worked seasonally so that she could spend the summer months with her children. She was serious about her mothering and had set standards based on her reaction to her own childhood troubles. She was determined that, unlike herself, her children would 'have a childhood.' She had also resolved to protect her children from physical punishment and abuse. Acting in a manner consistent with that objective, she left the security of her second marriage when she discovered that the children's father had abused one of them.

Marianne structured her choices around her children's needs and wishes: after separating from her husband, she commuted to work thirty-five miles every day so that they could remain in the familiar surroundings of their home town. Arlene, who was unable to ask for anything for herself, wanted to be sure her daughter didn't experience the deprivation she had felt as a child (this despite her overall recollection that her family had not been materially deprived). Jacqueline's sense of obligation to her family hinged on her belief that she had to comply with their requests.

Relations of Power

The lawbreaking actions of four of the women were directly influenced either by individuals – men – who held power over them or by social structures that were unresponsive to their individual needs, or both.

When the father of Rose's children ceased to contribute to their maintenance, Rose was unable to make ends meet on government assistance and turned to prostitution to supplement her welfare income. She was arrested on a charge of communicating for the purposes of prostitution by an undercover police officer who denied that he was a police officer when she asked. The fact that he lied apparently made no difference in the judicial proceedings that followed. Rose also encountered difficulties with the welfare system. She said that her heavy involvement with cocaine led to the termination of her welfare assistance,[1] forcing her back onto the streets in order to feed her children.

Marianne's husband was able to use the legal system to his advantage. (Marianne felt that the legal system was effectively accessible only to those who could afford to pay.) Still, Marianne might have been able to maintain her children without her ex-husband's support if she had been paid a living wage; her years of service and her level of competence certainly warranted such a wage. Rather than paying her what she deserved, however, her employer apparently chose to avoid his responsibility to her as an employee, and abused his power in the employer–employee relationship. He benefited from her dedication to him but felt no obligation to pay her accordingly. Marianne was distressed that both her husband and her employer were able to continue to live their lives with impunity, while she lost everything. She was also upset because she believed that her unscrupulous stepfather had deprived her of an inheritance from her mother that might have eased her situation. She was angry at the men and at the system that she found so inequitable.

Connie, too, came face to face with what she perceived to be an inequitable system. When she was most in need, the social services bureaucracy failed to provide adequate help. At another time, the client who purchased her bookkeeping services abused his power by threatening to take his business elsewhere unless she complied with his illegal request.

Although she maintained that her father's intentions were honourable, it seems that he, too, exploited Connie. He borrowed the money she received in the settlement of her divorce from her first husband, and repaid less than half of it. She justified lending him the money, saying that she did not need it at the time because she was working at two jobs; she also justified his request, saying that he had promised to return the money whenever she needed it. In the end, however, her father committed suicide, and she never recovered the balance of her money.

As in the case of the others, Arlene's lawbreaking could be linked to both a system and a man. Her job as a clerical worker was the least secure in the company that employed her. Once she was laid off, she had to face an unyielding welfare system that was unsympathetic even to a pregnant mother. Finally, she was approached outside the welfare office by a drug dealer whose sole purpose was to use her vulnerability to his own advantage. Moreover, Arlene felt that the method was tailored to the mark: she said, 'The guys that approach these girls, they know exactly what they're doing ... they know how to do it to make them want to do it.'

Jacqueline was forced to deal with a family system in which she became the outlet for a hostility that originated in the relationship in which she had been conceived. Her mother, possibly reminded by Jacqueline's very presence of a man whom she resented and a relationship that had failed, joined with her stepfather in making her a scapegoat.

LINKING NEED AND LAWBREAKING

The discourse on the link between social class and crime has been extensive and controversial. The views are disparate and usually organized by discipline: sociologists tend to emphasize the link and psychologists tend to dispute it.[2] The discussion is complicated by the fact that either the social class of origin or the socioeconomic status of the adult lawbreaker may be an important factor when individuals came into conflict with the law, or it may be that both or neither is important.

Relatively recently, feminists entered the fray and postulated a connection between women's poverty and women's lawbreaking. In their work with inmates, Adelberg and Currie[3] found that most of the women in Canadian prisons are poor. Speakers at the 1991 National Symposium on Women, Law, and the Administration of Justice emphasized a link between women's poverty and lawbreaking.[4] However, it is not clear how the speakers' assessments of socioeconomic status were carried out or whether they believed that poverty was always or frequently the motive for lawbreaking.

In a review of studies of crime in various socioeconomic groups, Carlen concluded that 'law-breaking is evenly distributed throughout all social classes,' and that 'a majority of law-breakers from *all* social classes can expect to escape penal regulation altogether.'[5] Yet, Carlen found that even when gender differences in patterns of lawbreaking are taken into account, it is women from lower socioeconomic groups that are more liable to criminalization than women from other socioeconomic groups. Thus, the issue seems to be not necessarily that women of lower social status are more likely to break the law, but that they are more likely to be criminalized through the justice system, which explains the observation that most women in prison are poor.

Gabor suggested that 'very few' individuals suffer the 'absolute deprivation' that might 'evoke a visceral response, through criminal behaviour, to ameliorate the situation.'[6] Certainly, although participants in the present study who explained their lawbreaking as related to 'need' were in situations that could be described as precarious at best, they had not experienced the extreme degree of personal deprivation to which Gabor refers. More to the point, four of those participants had children to support, a factor that rarely surfaces in the discourse on social class and crime (an omission that is perhaps attributable to the paucity of research studies about women). The women's concern was not with their own personal neediness or the neediness of their family of origin, but primarily with the fact that their *children* would be deprived if they did not provide adequately for them. None the less, their reactions do seem somewhat extreme, since the children were clearly not close to starvation. Despite her independence, Arlene said she could always go to her mother for food – and she sometimes did. Moreover, it is extremely difficult for landlords to evict mothers with children.

It can be argued that the women were projecting their sense of what had been missing from their own early family life onto their children – in their desire for them to 'have a childhood,' or to be able to enjoy a lifestyle similar to that of their friends. Like the women in Carlen's study who said they wanted their children to have the best, the four women in the present study wanted to prevent the retrogression of their children's socioeconomic status.[7] There is no doubt that the women regretted their own troubled childhoods and wanted better lives for their children, but that is no more than most parents want. Moreover, in attempting to meet their children's needs, the women were responding to them empathically. In my discussion of relational development theory, I indicated that parents' responsiveness is a crucial component in children's development. However, at the critical juncture between parental responsiveness and limitations, consumerism becomes a factor for consideration because of its power to distort the concept of need.

It seems that, like most of society, the women internalized what Caplan referred to as the myth that 'mothers are endless founts of nurturance.'[8] This myth is entrenched to the extent that women identify themselves as nurturers and are labelled deviant if they are perceived as inadequate in a nurturing role. Marianne, for example, began to doubt her own motives. She wondered whether she had taken the money for her children or herself, even though she had spent it to maintain their home and lifestyle. As she said, she had not spent the money on drugs or alcohol, and she did not own furs or jewels. The car she used to commute to work every day was ten years old. She wanted to do for her children the things that most parents want to do. However, she was caught in a low-paying job and deprived by her former husband of the child support to which the court said she was entitled; consequently, she was unable to be the 'endless fount' that society expects mothers to be. Even so, it seems that she doubted her own motives because she was unable to give her children everything she believed they needed.

Caplan pointed out that 'nurturing involves making the other person's life better – and women's power to do that is limited.'[9] Moreover, nurturing in the context of an ethic of consumerism is a formidable task indeed. Social expectations of mothers who are poor and single are no different from those of mothers who are rich and married. Poor, single mothers are expected to be emotionally and physically nurturing, and to provide all the 'goodies' that their children, like the children of wealthier parents, see on television or hear about in the school yard. However, powerful members of society do not necessarily see fit to ensure that all mothers are given similar opportunities to meet their children's needs and desires, many of which are created through the influence of a society oriented towards consumerism. Moreover, as long as women are denied pay equity and opportunities that are truly equal and supported by competent child care, and as long as they continue to be exploited by unscrupulous and powerful employers, they will be unable to meet those needs. Inevitably, some will attempt to compensate by following the route taken by Marianne, Rose, Arlene, and Connie.

Unlike the others, Jacqueline had no children to support or to nurture, but her story is no less affected by the values of a consuming society. Her story hinges on her relationship with her mother, a relationship characterized by role reversal. As a child, she was not nurtured by her mother, but was left in the care of her grandmother and an aunt, who did provide caring relationships for her. When she was very young, however, Jacqueline was removed from this nurturing environment and taken to live a frightening, unstable, and comfortless life with a mother and stepfather who were strangers to her. Although her physical needs were being adequately met, she was not nurtured; indeed, she gradually became the household's main provider of domestic labour and child care. Furthermore, the transition involved her removal from a Black community in another country to a White community in Canada, where she was forced by her White stepfather to attend a secondary school in which she was one of only a handful of Black students. Her sense of being different and the burden of her duties at home prevented her from integrating into the school, and added to her misery.

Jacqueline's situation is not unusual, in that Black women are often taught to be self-reliant and are expected to care for others in addition to earning a living. However, Turner suggests that in addition to teaching self-reliance, Black mothers often have a greater sense of responsibility to their daughters than do White mothers because of the adversities they experience in connection with both their race and their sex.[10] Unfortunately, Jacqueline could not enjoy such a relationship – one of loving co-conspiracy – with her mother. During the long periods of her mother's absence, she depended on her grandmother and aunt for a nurturing environment. Although her mother visited her grandmother's house intermittently, those visits were never sufficiently long or frequent to allow for the development of a mutually satisfactory mother–daughter relationship. As a result, Jacqueline never learned how to respond to her mother. Moreover, the situation only worsened when Jacqueline was taken from her nurturing environment to live with her mother and first one, then another, stepfather, and with the arrival of her half-sisters.

Jacqueline and her half-sisters were fathered by three different men. Only the first, Jacqueline's father, was a Black man; the other two were White. Jacqueline frequently remarked that she looked different from her sisters; that she, in fact, more closely resembled her mother than did her sisters, whereas they looked as though they might have been fathered by the same (White) man. Jacqueline was also treated differently. She was the family 'maid' – the person who was always missing from family pictures. Whether or not her stepfather and her mother were acting out of racism and internalized racism, respectively, is unclear, but this remains a possibility. What is clear is that Jacqueline felt that they had scapegoated her for reasons related to her paternity. Rather than nurturing the daughter who most resembled her, Jacqueline's mother failed to provide her with the sense of belonging that Jacqueline had felt in her relationships with her grandmother and her aunt.

When discussing the money she took, Jacqueline denied wanting an abundance of anything. She said, simply, 'I just wanted to be comfortable.' At the time, she was referring to material comfort, but her statement applies equally to her emotional involvement with her family. She really wanted only to be comfortable with them, and she had come to perceive her ability to be financially independent and to give her family gifts as her only means of attaining that level of comfort.

RETHINKING NEED

It is striking that the expectations of these women by their families were the antithesis of what was usually expected of women in White society – that they be passive and dependent. Three of the women are Black, and, as noted above, encouragement towards independence would not be considered unusual in their case.[11] However, the experiences of Connie and Marianne were not consistent with the guiding fiction that White women do not need to work, which is still prominent in some social spheres. For all five women, the expectation that they be independent was uninformed by social realities or by the reality of their individual qualifications and situations. They were expected, and believed that they should be able, to provide for themselves and their children even in the absence of social and family supports. For Marianne, her eventual inability to meet such demands brought about the disastrous result that she had long tried to avoid – having to hand her children over to their father and stepmother.

The conflict between family expectations and the real limitations in our society on women's earning power is a catch-22 familiar to many single mothers. The children of single mothers are expected to be every bit as presentable, in every way, as the children of two parents in a heterosexual union, despite the fact that single mothers must usually meet those expectations with very little assistance and with much less money than is available in a male-centred family. For women struggling to hold on to their children, the options for meeting the inherent challenges can be extremely limited, and very distressing.

For Jacqueline, the salient issues were, overtly, acceptance and belonging. Moreover, the efforts of all the women to conform to social and family expectations reflected the degree to which they desired acceptance and belonging. All the women suffered some sort of disconnection from their mothers, and from their fathers, and, as a result of their experiences, all were determined to maintain good relationships with their children. The message they got from society was that a good relationship with their children would consist, at least in part, of providing them with material goods.

It is apparent from the stories of these women that, when women's concerns are taken into account, the discourse concerning social class and socioeconomic status must be refocused. Simply to investigate a linear causality between deprivation, as a function of social class, and lawbreaking is to miss the point that, for women, monetary gain either for its own sake or for self-aggrandizement is rarely the issue. It is relevant, however, to examine how women have to struggle to maintain a consistent level of economic and emotional security for their children. It is also relevant to consider the cost to a woman of becoming and remaining acceptable in terms of familial and social expectations.

4

The Women's Words: Disconnection and the Influence of Others

Doreen and Bonnie said that their mothers were responsible for their conflicts with the law. As they related their stories, it became evident that they meant that a *disconnection* from their mothers had eventually led to their lawbreaking activity. Describing a situation similarly involving disconnection, Margaret said that her baby's death was responsible for her problems. Penny implicated a situation that involved disconnection from both her parents – their divorce – as a critical factor in her conflict with the law. Sarah named drugs, money, and the influence of persons whom she loved. As with the others, the threat of disconnection had always been present in her life, and many of her actions were determined by a longing for connection. All these women experienced loss of and disconnection from important people in their lives, either permanently or over extended periods of time.

Miller defines a sense of disconnection as occurring 'when a child or adult is prevented from participating in mutually responsive and mutually enhancing relationships.' She states that 'disconnections occur when the child or adult is grossly abused or attacked, when the surrounding relational context is unresponsive to the child or adult's expression of her experience, or, as is usually the case, when both of these occur simultaneously.'[1] Miller also postulates, however, that everyone experiences many small disconnections throughout life that do not lead to serious problems and that contribute to the growth process as long as many 'enlarging' connections are experienced as well. Miller did not discuss methods for determining a growth-promoting balance of disconnections and connections, and it is doubtful that such a balance can be struck 'objectively.' Rather, the balance is sensed internally, or subjectively.

The women whose stories are told in this chapter experienced many serious disconnections, with which they had to cope in isolation from responsive others. According to Miller, 'the most terrifying and destructive feeling that a person can experience is isolation' – that is, an isolation in which the woman feels locked out of the possibility of human connection.[2] Through their stories, the women told me that they experienced exactly that sort of isolation.

BONNIE

Bonnie, a twenty-one-year-old Caucasian woman, declared that responsibility for the direction of her life and her conflicts with the law lay with her mother, the institutions in which she grew up, and the abuse that riddled her life.

I'd like to relive it. Live in a home, not in group homes ... because I wouldn't be in this situation if I didn't live in a group home and receiving homes and foster homes ... I wouldn't know about the law, I wouldn't get in trouble. I'd still be in school, probably college right now. It's all my mother's fault really. She put me in Children's Aid, different schools ...

Bonnie recalled that, when she was two years old, she had fallen down the stairs in her home and broken both her legs. Although she was confused about the details of the incident, Bonnie thought her mother was drunk at the time and must have given her a push, which made her fall. She said, 'I'm not really putting the blame on my mom, but I think it was my mom who damaged me up like that.' As noted earlier, Miller states that one way in which disconnections can occur is through abuse. Thus, Bonnie's disconnection from her mother may have begun before she was removed from her home by the Children's Aid Society (CAS).

Bonnie said she lived in foster homes, group homes, and receiving homes until she was sixteen. She was a frequent runaway from these homes, especially in her early teens. Although she remembered some of them as good homes, and lived in one for three years, her overall experience of them was not positive. She said she did not have a childhood. She began to break the law when she was as young as age six or seven; she would shoplift candy and other treats because she never had any money but wanted to have candy, like the other children she knew. She said that one of the things that bothered her most about her life was that she had not been raised 'in a home.' Although she regretted that she had lost touch with her siblings and that she had never had a close relationship with her mother, her regret went beyond not having been raised by her own family: Bonnie felt that she would have been better off if she had been able to stay in one place, to grow up in a single, consistent, home.

My mom should've just given me up instead of keeping me in Children's Aid – in and out, in and out, in and out, in and out. Too much of a stress on me not knowing what was going on, different homes. I remember one very nice home I was in – very nice, but it was all so – like – I was in one group home or foster home and then out again ... I been in so many different schools I don't even remember anymore.

Not surprisingly, Bonnie's education suffered and her resulting inability to read well was a source of embarrassment. It made her 'feel stupid about things.'

Ideally, Bonnie felt that she would have been better off if she had been raised by her mother and her 'real' father. She believed that the man who her mother insisted was her father was actually her stepfather, and she claimed to know nothing about her biological father. Her mother and stepfather beat her with a belt, and they fought each other 'a lot' when she was growing up. Bonnie remembered always feeling that they were fighting about her. She felt that her mother would never leave her step-father because he supported the family financially.

Although Bonnie was in the care of the CAS, her mother and stepfather took her home for visits, and it was during those visits that her stepfather began to abuse her sexually. From the time she was seven years old, her stepfather forced her to have intercourse with him, and he fathered the first two of her five children when she was fourteen and fifteen years old. At different times, Bonnie said both that she did not remember the actual first incident of abuse and that she would never forget it; she knew it had happened because there was blood on the sheets. Bonnie said she could not remember the details of the abuse, which suggested that, in all prob-ability, she had learned to dissociate while she was being abused. Practi-tioners and researchers working with survivors of sexual abuse have found that dissociation is not uncommon among them.[3] Bonnie declared that she didn't remember 'because I don't want the memory brought back.' She said, 'I don't want to find out about a lot of stuff, so I keep it locked inside.' It seemed that suppression was her way of protecting herself, be-cause she said of her 'barrier' that 'once somebody breaks that down, I go off' (by which she meant that she would bang her head on the floor or become suicidal). Bonnie was also sexually abused by her mother's brothers, an experience she remembered with some pleasure because she felt that they had taught her about 'the birds and the bees' and had treated her well. Because of their distant relationship, Bonnie never told her mother about the sexual abuse. She recalled that, on one occasion, her mother had asked her if her stepfather touched her. Rather than hurt her mother's feelings, Bonnie simply turned and walked away. None the less, she thought that her mother knew the truth.

She doesn't want to believe it but she sort of believes it because she used to ask me when I was a kid, 'How come you don't like Richard?' And I said, 'There's no reason, I just don't like him.' And then she says, 'Does he touch you?' Then I would walk away when she said that. So obviously she must've known.

Later, Bonnie said that 'she [her mother] more or less knew [about the abuse], because I told her.'

Whether or not her mother knew of the abuse, she and Bonnie never discussed it openly. Neither did Bonnie discuss her first two pregnancies with her mother; she thought her mother didn't know about them, which seems unlikely. It seems that Bonnie's mother colluded with her in a conspiracy of silence about the abuse and thus ignored the pregnancies, perhaps because she and her three younger children were financially dependent on Richard. Although it seems preposterous that her mother could have ignored something as obvious as a pregnant daughter, Bonnie said that, at the time, she was living in group homes and saw her mother infrequently. She also said that she was very heavy at the time, so that her changing shape was less noticeable than it might otherwise have been.

Bonnie seemed to understand that her mother was not able to acknowledge the pregnancies. She seemed to be denying anger at her mother in order to maintain their relationship, such as it was.

No, because she – I have to forgive her like she has to forgive me for what I've done. I'm not angry at her ... because I understand. She loves the guy. I think she loves him because of the money, to be honest with you. And that's OK, because if she gets all that money it's going to go to all us kids anyway.

Although Bonnie purported to understand her mother, her mother's lack of support amounted to another disconnection. As noted earlier, Miller states that disconnections occur when a person is abused, when the person's relational context is unresponsive, or when both those things occur simultaneously. In thinking that she would inherit money from her mother, Bonnie may have been hoping for connection through a response to her needs, even if only to future material needs.

In theories of development, the effect of the child on the parent is rarely considered, because it is assumed that, when a person becomes a parent, she has reached an adult stage of development that is not amenable to changes as a result of the birth and continuing presence of a child. However, when the parent is still a child herself, it is especially important to consider the developmental changes precipitated by pregnancy and the birth of a child. Although Bonnie said little about the first two pregnancies, the last three presented opportunities to form a connection with her mother. However, the matter was complicated by the fact that she lost all five of the children she had borne. Her first child died at birth. The second and third were adopted out at birth, and the fourth was taken by the CAS when she was about two months old, after she had been severely abused. (Bonnie said that her husband had abused both her and the baby, but she was charged in connection with the abuse as well. She denied the charge.) The fifth child was taken from the hospital by the CAS following his birth. Understanding the effect on Bonnie of having been pregnant for almost four of her twenty-one years, and of having lost five children, is critical to understanding Bonnie.

In studies of women who have lost children through stillbirth or miscarriage, it has been found that the women experienced greater self-denigration than with other types of losses, and that they experienced guilt as well as anger at having been cheated.[4] For Bonnie, the loss of her children was undoubtedly exceptionally traumatic, because she herself was still a child, or adolescent, when she gave birth to and lost her first three children. Moreover, she had no essential, empathic relationship to help her through the losses of her children. Although only one of her children was lost through perinatal death, the others were lost at birth or very soon after, through adoption. Judging from Bonnie's account of events and from her reaction to the loss of her most recent child to the CAS, which occurred between our first and second interviews, it seemed that, after the loss of each child, Bonnie protested vehemently, but to no avail. The usual advice Bonnie received from hospital, agency, and institutional representatives was that she should try to 'get over' the loss of the child as quickly as possible. However, for Bonnie, this advice had the effect of negating her experience of loss, effectively making her loss a 'non-event.'[5] Under the circumstances, probably the safest thing for her to do, in terms of her emotional state, was to deny any feelings about the events. This is precisely what she did, after creating an initial uproar. Very likely, this process was similar to her experience with her other losses.

Leon states that 'first and foremost, perinatal death is a narcissistic loss for the mother,' because it is as though she has lost a part of herself, not a separate individual.[6] For Bonnie, the loss of her children was more complex because of the nature of the interaction between her and her mother during her pregnancies. Bonnie's mother did not acknowledge the first two pregnancies, but renewed her interest in Bonnie with each of the last three. Bonnie suspected that her mother was drawn to her only because of the expected babies, but she seemed to accept the connection, regardless of her mother's motivation. From her mother's perspective, the pregnancies may have been the only common ground she could find on which to forge a connection with a daughter who was an unknown to her. Thus, Bonnie's pregnancies provided a medium through which mother and daughter could, however briefly, connect at some level of mutual understanding. Consequently, however, because her mother's interest in her waned with the loss of each baby, Bonnie not only experienced the loss of her children but also re-experienced the initial loss of her mother. In the framework of a theory of relational development which holds that a mutually empathic relationship is essential to the foundation of a core self-structure, Bonnie repeatedly lost the opportunity to confirm her ability to connect within relationship each time she experienced the loss of her mother.

When I asked Bonnie how she felt about having given birth to, then losing, five children, her response was typical of others she had given in response to emotionally laden questions – flippant and devoid of affect. She simply said, 'I have to live with it, not anybody else,' and 'You get used to it.' Bonnie coped in the same way with the hurt she felt in her relationship with her mother. She said, 'I have to live with it. Nobody else does. I'm sort of beginning to cope with her, understanding her. I can't do nothing about it.' However, in other moments, Bonnie allowed some vulnerability to show. She said, 'It may not look it, but inside I hurt.'

Bonnie's attempts to 'understand' her mother, her inability to trust, and her lack of affect when discussing painful issues were suggestive to me of someone who is fearful of losing something or someone, and who feels she cannot afford the risk of appearing vulnerable. Her interactions with me during the interviews confirmed those impressions. Most telling was the following incident: It was difficult to produce audible tapes of the interviews because of noise from the hallway outside my office, so I had to keep the door of the small room tightly closed. Bonnie felt uncomfortable with this arrangement but was afraid to ask to have the door left open. Only after telling another inmate about it and being encouraged to ask did she muster the courage to ask me to leave the door slightly ajar. Since participation in the research was strictly voluntary, Bonnie could have avoided the issue entirely by simply refusing to return for the second interview. She did return and was apparently getting something from the process – hopefully an empathic connection – that she was reluctant to relinquish. Even so, she couldn't let herself trust me enough to ask me to provide the situation she needed in order to feel comfortable, until she was reassured by a trusted inmate who had been coming to me for counselling that I would not be offended by the request. It seemed that she desired the connection with me and did not want to jeopardize it; consequently, when the situation was uncomfortable for her, she initially sacrificed her own needs rather than risk severing the connection.

When Bonnie was sixteen, she was released from agency involvement and left to fend for herself. She thus lost even the minimal 'connection' of familiar, ongoing involvement with agencies. She was semi-literate and had no marketable skills. Influenced by her peers, she began to use soft drugs and, on one occasion, 'needled' cocaine. She also 'became an alcoholic.' When she was eighteen, she stopped using alcohol, but her husband re-introduced her to cocaine, and it became her drug of choice: 'I tried 'basing. I liked it and I constantly went at it.' To supplement her small welfare income, she worked at low-paying jobs in fast-food restaurants. However, a girl she met told her it was 'easy' to make money as a prostitute, so she took up the trade to pay for 'rent, food, drugs – like hash and weed, alcohol.' Between her eighteenth birthday and the time she and I met, she had been incarcerated twice. Bonnie did not regret her prostitution, saying 'it's not against the law to sell your body.' On the contrary, she found prostitution exciting because she met 'weird people.'

Bonnie's drug and alcohol use may be understood in connection with her need to protect herself from the pain of her losses, and her desire to form relationships with other people. On the one hand, the behaviour was consistent with her tendency to protect herself from strong feelings by blocking them: drug use temporarily protected her from experiencing the pain of recurrent disconnections. On the other hand, it allowed her some contact with other people, however superficial and ultimately destructive that contact often turned out to be.

For Bonnie, the inordinate number of disconnections and losses in her young life had a drastic outcome. She said, 'I hate my life that I have lived,' and 'It's like I feel I don't exist to anybody, for Christmas, birthdays, nothing. I feel like I don't exist.'

MARGARET

Until Margaret was about seven, her mother raised the family of seven children largely on her own. Margaret's sisters were married with families, and her surviving brothers held good jobs. One brother hanged himself when Margaret was twenty-eight.

When she was a child, Margaret's father usually worked out of town as a logger, and would be gone for long periods of time. When he changed jobs and started working steadily in a new city, the family joined him and stayed there.

Although she had respect for both parents, Margaret, a thirty-five-year-old Caucasian woman, said they gave her two different kinds of upbringings. Her mother worked outside the home, cleaned, took care of the children, and ironed their face cloths, their pyjamas, and their socks. 'She was there; she was a fanatic in a way.' Margaret did not feel that her emotional needs were met by her mother, who favoured Margaret's younger brother. Margaret felt her mother gave up being a mother after her first three children were born (and before Margaret was born) because she wanted to be out working, although she did continue to be an efficient housekeeper and provider. Margaret interpreted this with sympathy, saying that she felt her mother needed time for herself. She said her mother's 'only fault' was that she 'didn't spend enough time with certain kids.'

Although Margaret respected her mother, one incident stood out in her mind as a great disappointment. It had to do with her leaving one friend to play with another:

This bothered me to no end. I was always taught to play at not just one friend. Let other people be friends too. But my mother got mad because I wanted to play with another little girl down the street. Nobody wanted to play with that kid because they were poor, and I didn't think that was any reason not to play with her, so I said to my friend, 'If you want to come play, come play, and if you don't, don't, but I'm going to play.' Well, that went back to my mother, and I got a lecture on – 'You shouldn't leave your friend to go play with another friend.'

To the day of our interview, the incident bothered Margaret, because her mother had always taught her to share. To Margaret, sharing meant that she had to be with more than one person, so she felt that her mother was contradicting not only her own teaching, but also what her father had taught her and her siblings. She said, 'It seemed like she was trying to impress my friend's mother.' Most important, perhaps, was Margaret's sense that her mother had made her appear to be wrong in order to placate her friend's mother. For Margaret, this was a serious breach of an already tenuous connection, a connection that had apparently survived on the strength of Margaret's belief in her parents' teachings, and her attempts to follow them. For the connection to be a viable one, Margaret had to believe that her parents respected her efforts to live by their teachings; in other words, she needed to have a sense of their responsiveness to her efforts.

Perhaps because her emotional needs could not be met by her overburdened mother, or perhaps because her father had been absent from her life for so long, Margaret tended to idealize her father. Margaret thought he was a loner, probably an alcoholic, and her mother told her that he had 'fooled around.' None the less, Margaret felt that her father had taught her important lessons. She remembered him as a very giving person who would encourage her and her siblings to sit down and talk with people if they were having problems. She believed that her own tendency to be accommodating to other people was based on her father's example:

I think it's the way my dad raised us ... you remember to put somebody in that looked different from us ... if they had a problem, sit down and talk to that person ... my father seemed to adopt everything and anything. If it walked on four legs, it was welcome, too.

Margaret denied that her father's tendency to bring people home reduced the amount of attention that family members received, because 'I did my own thing. We all did our own thing.' It seems, then, that Margaret received nurturance from her father vicariously. When I pressed her about the issue of getting attention, it became evident that she had created a rationale for her sense of aloneness within the family, saying, 'but do you necessarily need that attention?' She went on to tell me how much she had always enjoyed her time alone, even as a child.

When her father was killed in a car accident, she felt a profound loss; even at the time of our interviews, she said that she still missed him. Only eleven when he died, she said that she felt 'a coldness, an emptiness' set in. She was unable to sleep at night unless she was comforted by her older sister. To make matters worse, her father's death resulted in another move, when her mother used his insurance to secure a better home.

Margaret 'flunked a couple of grades' early on because, she said, it was hard, when the family moved, to leave behind the teachers and friends whom she had liked. However, she enjoyed school until she got to junior high, when groups formed, and she 'slacked off.' She was something of an outsider at school, and she took up with a group of teenagers who were not attending school. They introduced her to alcohol, and she began to skip classes in favour of drinking home-made wine at a friend's. Because of her involvement with this group, her mother began to mistrust her, and this mistrust proved to be a turning point in Margaret's life.

When I was growing up, all the girls that I went around with were pregnant, or got pregnant. I was the only one, which made a lot of conflict between me and my mother, because she assumed I was doing the same things as they were doing, which I wasn't – and she didn't have the respect she should've had ... she didn't trust me ... and that sort of put a barrier between me and her, and that's why I left.

The issue of trust was very important to Margaret. Even though she and her mother had never been close, it was not until her mother began to mistrust her that Margaret felt there was a real barrier between them. Once that barrier was erected, Margaret could no longer live with her mother. She moved to another city, lived 'with street people' for several years, began to abuse drugs, and continued to abuse alcohol.

The loss of her mother's trust was intolerable for Margaret. She grew up in a family of loners; indeed, she described both her parents and herself as loners. In this milieu of separateness, Margaret forged an unusual connection: Judging by the importance she placed on being treated fairly by her parents, it seems that she embraced their exhortations on matters of fairness as her primary connection to them. Faced with a mother who could not provide her with a nurturing relationship, and with the loss of a father whom she had idealized but who had been essentially emotionally absent, Margaret clung instead to the lessons her parents had taught her. When her mother committed the inevitable human error of contradicting her own teaching, Margaret did not know how to respond. She seemed to regard her parents' teachings as a near-sacred trust, and for her to violate them would have been unthinkable. This was something she expected her mother to know about her. Consequently, when her mother failed to trust her, it was as though the last connection to her had been threatened. Margaret seemed to feel that, if she wanted to salvage the connection to her respected mother, her only recourse was to leave home. In effect, she sacrificed actual contact with the real person in order to protect what nurturance her mother had been able to give.

When we met, Margaret had been a drug abuser for seventeen years and said she had tried every drug available to her. Even so, she felt that the drugs had not taken over her life. She distinguished herself from severely dependent addicts by the fact that, unlike them, she did not need a 'rock' first think in the morning. Margaret began drinking home-made wine at a friend's house at age fifteen, and began smoking pot heavily when she left home. She experimented with many drugs, and speed became a favourite. She drank 'like a fish' for a long time, but had stopped drinking two years before our interviews. At about the same time, however, she started to use cocaine. She had been incarcerated only once before; both sentences were for drug-related offences.

Margaret said that she was not criminally minded and did not 'go out and break the law.' She said she had a 'really soft nature' and 'that's where I get in trouble.' She said she felt sorry for a lot of people, and didn't like to see kids teased or people ignored because they were different. She felt that if she said 'no' to people, she would be hurting their feelings. The charge for which she was incarcerated involved arranging a drug deal for a woman who had been living in her apartment. The woman had settled into Margaret's apartment with an assortment of other drug-users whom Margaret described as 'vegetables' and 'zombies.' The woman had been pestering Margaret to arrange the deal, and Margaret finally acquiesced 'in order to shut her up.'

Margaret was propelled into her most recent period of immersion in cocaine by the loss of her infant daughter, who died of crib death at the age of two months. The death of the baby, her first daughter – 'the one baby I wanted' – devastated Margaret, and she felt that all her problems resulted from it.

I wanted a new apartment – she died in my bed – and when she was born I was granted a new apartment. When she died I was denied it, which meant I still lived where she died. Feelings were still too close to – and I just died with her. I mean that's basically what my story was; I just died because I wanted her so bad.

She said, 'my daughter was me,' and when her daughter died, Margaret gave up and 'died' too. Before her daughter's death Margaret would make sure that bills were paid and that food had been bought before she would buy drugs, but afterwards, she began to neglect her two older children – boys, ages twelve and two – and didn't care about providing groceries or clean clothes.

And the other two, I loved them so much that I pushed them away. I didn't want to hurt them. I didn't want to be hurt. If anything ever happened to them, I'd be hurt all over again. So I pushed them away.

Margaret thought that if she'd gotten help or had had family support after her daughter's death, she might not have become so heavily involved in the drug culture.

Although her daughter's death was the most traumatic event she had ever experienced, Margaret suffered losses and disconnections much earlier in her life. She had limited resources and supports with which to manage her emotional reactions both to those early losses and disconnections and to her daughter's death.

PENNY

Penny, a Caucasian woman, was thirty-two years old at the time of the interviews. When I first asked her to talk about the experiences that brought her to jail, she said that she had initially been incarcerated because of her drug use. Later in our interviews, she said,

I always sit and think of why did I turn out the way I did turn out ... and everyone tries to blame it on my parents. But I don't blame it on my parents, I blame it on the situation.

The 'situation' to which Penny referred was her parents' divorce, which took place when she was ten years old. It did, indeed, seem to be a pivotal event in her life.

If anything happened to me when I was a child – something bad or maybe something that would make me do the drugs I do, or do whatever I do – I don't remember. 'Cause all I remember is everything being good. Except for my mom and dad breaking up. I hated that part. I took it a lot worse than my sister did ... I just couldn't understand it. Why they wouldn't want to live together ... because everything was so good and then all of a sudden it just ...

In fact, everything had not been 'so good.' There had been considerable upheaval in the family prior to the divorce. Penny recalled that her parents would fight when they were drinking on weekends. 'I could hear them arguing and – behind a door and you could hear my dad smack her.' She found her parents' fighting disturbing, and she tried to stop it.

I hated it. I remember when I was young I used to run away, but I wouldn't run far. I'd run down the street and hide in the bushes because they were fighting ... I was wishing they would stop, and if I ran away, maybe they would think about stopping ...

Penny and her sister would talk and cry together about their parents' fights. Sometimes they involved themselves in the fights, rushing to their mother's defence.

I remember them fighting a lot. A few times I remember they were physically fighting and I'd get right in there. I was just young but I remember getting in the middle, trying to stop it ... I remember my dad smacking my mom – in the living room ... It wasn't like he was punching her out or anything, he just gave her a few smacks and I jumped on my dad's back to stop him.

Both of Penny's parents were always employed, in blue-collar, sales, or clerical jobs, and she and her sister, who was two years older, were cared for by nannies, of whom she has little memory. Her mother's continual 'bitching' would push Penny to the point of wanting to hit her. To add to her frustration, her father always had to have the last word on every-thing.

When Penny was eight or nine years old, the family moved to the United States, because her father had taken a job there. Penny said, 'I was angry they took me away from school with all my friends and I had to go start all over again.' To add to her distress, race riots were taking place in the city to which they had moved. Penny also recalled that the children in her class made fun of her accent. Her mother hated the city, and they returned to Canada after a year or so, but the family had changed. Her parents had separated in the United States. When they moved back to Canada, Penny and her sister stayed with their mother.

Despite the problems, Penny remembered happy times spent together as a family during those ten years, which seemed to compensate for the pain and which made those years seem 'good,' especially in retrospect. Consequently, she was very upset by the news of her parents' divorce. She found it really 'scary,' packed a suitcase, and ran away and hid in the bushes down the street from her house. The separation was the major loss of her life, and, after it happened, Penny never really settled into a 'nor-mal' life. Although she still saw her father, she felt she had lost him. His departure was especially painful for her because she had felt very close to him when she was younger, and she identified with him. She said that she was very much like him in attitude and appearance. Penny was also similar to her father in that she would hit her mother if her mother tried to spank her. She was less well behaved than her sister, but she was also the favourite, and when she was little, her misbehaviour was considered 'cute.' Penny said that she had been a 'big girl' with a 'bad temper.' Penny's actions during the period following her parents' divorce were suggestive of someone attempting either to draw attention to her distress or to gain some control over the situation itself. By the age of twelve, Penny was running away from home, staying out all night, and stealing to get 'nice things.' If her behaviour was a ploy to reunite her parents, as it had been a ploy to stop their fighting in her earlier years, it worked temporarily. When Penny returned home in the morning, her mother would call her father, who would come and administer discipline, usually in the form of 'grounding,' because her mother was unable to handle her. Of course, her efforts to reunite her parents did not succeed (if, indeed, that was her aim).

To compound Penny's losses, her sister left home. Although she and her sister had often fought physically, 'over clothes and stuff,' Penny regretted her leaving. Penny always had friends around, but, she said, 'it's not the same as having your family.' With her sister's departure, Penny was left with her mother and her mother's male friend, to whom she referred as an 'idiot' and whose presence she found offensive. 'He used to beat my mom up, too. I'd come in and see it ... oh! I'd just go crazy.'

In the midst of the tumultuous events of her life, Penny searched for companionship and comfort wherever she could find them. She began to experiment with drugs, eager to try anything that was available. She remembered trying LSD at the age of thirteen, and she started 'needling' speed. Perhaps this, too, was a plea for someone to notice and deal with her distress, for she left syringes in places in the house where they could easily be spotted by her mother and her mother's male companion. Penny said, 'I don't think I wanted them to find them. I think I was just careless.'

When she became involved in stealing and drugs, her choices of friends became limited.

We're all a certain type of kid, where the good kids would never hang around with us because we'd go out and do those things. So if I didn't hang around with that crowd I would never had ended up this way, I don't think.

However, she had plunged into a cycle from which it became increasingly difficult to remove herself.

There were times in my life that I did change, though, and started taking the right track, and then I'd get – I don't know what it was, I'd just get bored or I'd want more excitement and I'd end up getting into trouble.

Having had a taste of excitement, and having cut herself off from the 'good' kids, Penny became absorbed in a lifestyle of lawbreaking. She quit school when she was fifteen and, with her mother's permission, moved into an apartment with some older people. She was introduced to heroin, which immediately became her drug of choice. By sixteen, she was addicted, and had been convicted of trafficking the drug. She said that sentences were usually light at that time, often only probation, and it wasn't until she was twenty-one that she was incarcerated for a substantial length of time. When we met, she was serving a sentence for dozens of charges related to her lifestyle. During the previous ten years, she hadn't been out of jail for longer than a year at a time. Penny thought of jail as the price she paid for the life she led.

At the heart of Penny's lawbreaking and the lifestyle she found exciting was her addiction to heroin. In order to supply her habit, Penny committed fraud, then moved on to prostitution when she was twenty-six, fearing that further arrests for fraud would lead to longer prison sentences. She would often steal credit cards from her 'tricks' (though not from her regular customers), especially those who haggled over the two or three hundred dollars that she charged. Penny also raised money by acquiring prens from physicians for drugs such as Percodan; she would have the prescriptions filled and sell the drugs. She found this work very challenging and would often use props such as phoney plaster casts to convince the physicians of her need for the painkillers. Penny said she still had a 'conscience,' however; for example, she wouldn't steal anyone's personal belongings, such as jewellery.

Although on occasion it had been dangerous, Penny liked prostitution, even though she didn't enjoy the sex. She thought 'it was great that a woman could make so much money doing something like that,' and she felt that she was unlike most women in that she could do it without using drugs (that is, without being high).

Penny's work paid off; she cited one four-month period in which she made $80,000. However, supporting her habit was a full-time job that required planning. (Penny once said that 'straightening out and having no job is just waiting for relapse,' because a heroin addict's days are so busy.) If she didn't plan, she'd do 'stupid things and end up in jail.' Also, every day, she'd have to be sure to have an adequate supply of the drug for the next morning, because she couldn't go out to work if she was sick from withdrawal, and she needed to work so that she could continue to buy the drug.

Asked how heroin made her feel, she smiled and became nostalgic as she recalled her first 'hit,' twenty years earlier:

You fall in love with the high. It's hard to explain. You just get really high. You can't – you feel like you're not in this – you're really relaxed. It's hard to explain – you have to experience it.

Although heroin could initially transport her into a world of painless-ness, the tables turned when she became addicted: 'after a while, you're not high any more, you're just normal.' Penny discovered the painful world of withdrawal – 'It's the worst thing you could ever go through, throwing up, diarrhea, you can't move' – and the cycle that would dom-inate the remaining years of her life established itself. Heroin became the organizing feature of Penny's life, and supplying her habit became a full-time job. The exigencies of a heroin addiction became the focal point of her life and, over the years, did as much to help Penny avoid emotional pain as did the effects of the drug itself. Moreover, she could always count on drugs to fill the empty spots in her life:

You're sitting at home and you go, 'Ah, I'd like to get high right now.' And no one's there. You're just sitting by yourself, you've got no one to talk to. You just go out and get high. It's as easy as that.

SARAH

Sarah, age twenty-four, described herself as a good, honest person, strong-minded and independent. She said she knew how to take care of herself and other people. She said she was 'not very good at pointing out [her] negative side.'

I understood Sarah's story best within the context of my own reactions to her and of her reactions to the interview process. Sensing some discom-fort at the end of the first interview, I asked what it was like for her to be discussing her life with me. She responded that it was 'embarrassing ... 'cause I'm worried about what you're going to think about me when I see you later, in the hallways or whatever.'

Sarah's need to appear in a favourable light was a reflection of her insecurity with other people, which seemed to have its origin in a chaotic and alienating family life. For her, childhood was both 'miserable' and 'funny.' She remembered some good things, such as a special gift at Christmas, the big house she once lived in, coming home to music playing and her mother's cooking, and a woman named Maggie – a 'second mother' – who had been hired to help her mother with the house and children. Maggie's departure to raise her own family, when Sarah was about nine years old, was a loss for Sarah.

Sarah's mother was part Aboriginal Canadian, and Sarah prided herself on being Métis. Sarah, who was the penultimate child of eight, longed to be friends with her siblings, and the 'miserable side' of her childhood consisted of not being allowed to tag along with them. When any of them showed her some attention, she was delighted. Getting attention often meant cooperating with her siblings – usually her brothers – in ways that her parents would not have approved. Sarah was a source of amusement for her brothers; they would give her marijuana and watch her reaction.

I got started using it from my older brothers, actually. ... I remember when I was ten years old, they'd get me stoned, you know, and laugh at me ... but I mean ... they weren't – it wasn't anything serious. It was just for a joke. They were young, too; they were only sixteen and fifteen.

Her eagerness to be included made her vulnerable to her brother Jason, who was a strong influence in Sarah's life. He was wild as a boy and was sent to training school when he was ten years old. By the time he was twenty-eight, he had spent fifteen years in jail or 'juvies' (detention centres for juveniles). Sarah said Jason was the biggest problem in the family. There was 'always something happening with him.' However, Sarah remembered that she looked up to Jason 'very much' when she was younger. 'I used to think he was cool ... he was, too. He had a car always; he always had money ... just his style. If you know him, he's really neat. Back then, I used to follow him.' She also won favour with Jason by helping him with his heists.

He made me do stuff when I was younger. He used to – he'd rob a place, a house, and he'd take me with him, and I was like, nine years old, and he used to bring me in the house and [I'd] help him carry out stuff from the house.

Loyalty to Jason meant being deceitful with her mother. 'I knew it was wrong and I never told my mom, but that's the first time I ever broke the law. It was from him.' Later, she started 'doing it on my own,' and then she would shoplift clothes.

It was hardly surprising, considering the details of Sarah's story, that her activities with Jason went undetected by her parents. Sarah's father was an alcoholic who was either physically or functionally absent from the family most of the time. When he was present, he sometimes sabotaged her mother's efforts to manage the large family. Sometimes both parents would be drinking, and it reached the point where Sarah did not want to come home after school because she 'didn't want to see anything that might be happening there.'

Sarah's mother was the primary administrator of discipline, which took the form of spankings. If Sarah was late coming home, she was beaten, although she said she wasn't abused. When this happened at the age of fifteen, Sarah ran away. She returned three months later and was never disciplined again; in fact, she said she always did pretty much as she pleased. Sarah felt this lack of discipline was a source of her problems. Her father would spank the boys but not the girls, and he 'called all the kids "sweetheart." ' Sarah knew that if her mother denied her something, she could often get it from her father. Sarah thought she was like her father because they were both dependent on a form of drug, they both liked to take care of themselves and speak their minds, they both had a lot of love to give, and they both liked to take care of other people. Sarah said she and her younger sister were her father's 'prized possessions.'

Sarah's parents fought often, and her father occasionally beat her mother, throwing her off a balcony on one occasion. Her mother was always employed outside the home, and held a responsible supervisory job. Sarah remembered her mother being upset and worried, and her parents talking about money.

It wasn't a good feeling because mom was upset and I remember hearing them talk about stuff – money a lot – and I knew that she was worried.

Since her mother handled everything else, Sarah thought she should be able to control her father's drinking as well, even though her father was a very 'dominant' man.

I always heard her talking to my dad, you know, but I just ... I did hold it against her. I was mad at her, always, when that happened, and then I felt sorry for her because I was mad. But she'd never know I was mad at her half the time.

When the disruption of the family on a day-to-day basis could no longer be tolerated, Sarah's mother threatened to leave her father. Instead, the family moved to another town. They 'sold everything and moved away from those people [neighbours who had been drinking friends of her father's].' Sarah said that, to her, the move was exciting, but that her brothers were not pleased about it. However, she said the problems involved in the move were 'nothing that my mom couldn't handle. We were moving and that was it.'

Although she remembered her mother as being 'good,' Sarah never went straight to her mother with a problem, preferring to discuss it first with a sister, because she couldn't trust her mother to keep her matters confidential:

My mom's really open ... when she was concerned about one, everybody would know about it. So that's why I always heard about my brother Jason. My mom did always express how she was feeling.

Sarah was especially concerned about her mother talking to one of her older sisters, Mary, who, she felt, was jealous and critical of her:

I thought maybe my mom wouldn't understand ... I was scared to tell her things in case she ever said it in front of somebody, like my oldest sister, the one I didn't want to know.

Sarah did not trust Mary. When Sarah was in need of an abortion, she asked Mary to sign papers for her, and swore her to secrecy. However, Mary told their mother about the abortion, and Sarah was bitterly disappointed by her breach of confidence. The relationship never recovered; in fact, the rift between the two sisters was exacerbated by Sarah's mother and her other sisters, who reported to Sarah mean things that Mary said about her. Sarah, a very attractive woman, felt that Mary was jealous of her.

Sarah 'did excellent' at school, earning the 'athlete of the year' award several years in a row. However, she was very nervous about going to high school. She and her friends began to 'drink and smoke pot,' financing her habit with her allowance, as well as by baby-sitting and working in a store.

It affected my whole life but I didn't realize that until it was too late ... because after a while we were just smoking at lunchtime, and then we started smoking at lunchtime and after school, and then we'd not go to school and just go to someone's house and smoke up all day. Then we got into drinking beer on weekends and the same thing with that also – we started drinking every day and I just quit school when I was starting Grade 10. I quit going to school – I kept leaving my house – my mom didn't know I quit until a couple months later, but I never went to school after that.

When she was about nineteen or twenty, her situation deteriorated significantly as she became 'wired' to heroin; her involvement with the drug was Sarah's explanation for her lawbreaking. Her description of how the drug made her feel provided insight into both the way she experienced her life and her attraction to the drug:

... sleeping like a baby ... all your pain, everything, as soon as you do the heroin – it starts from your feet, right up, out of your head. Anything that's troubling you, any pain you may be feeling, it's gone.

Her initial experience of heroin remains in sharp contrast to what that experience was to become – the avoidance, at all costs, of the terrible sickness of withdrawal. Sarah had overdosed, but 'not very often – only about five times.'

When she first became addicted to heroin, Sarah sold cocaine to support her habit. Later, she began to manipulate everyone she knew – family, friends, acquaintances – for money. She said she 'always met too many people,' many of whom were rich and gave her things. It was during this period that she also became involved in 'scams' and prostitution. Her scam worked as follows: She would hitch-hike, asking the man who stopped if he wanted 'company.' When he parked the car, she would take his money, then either jump out of the car and run, or use some ploy to get away. A favourite ploy was to ask the man if he had a condom. If he said no, she would ask if he wanted to go buy one or if he wanted her to do it. She would then either run off from the store or abandon the car while the man was in the store. She called this work a 'business.'

Sarah was arrested several times for robbery as a result of this business operation, but she usually beat the charges in court, because it was ultimately her word against the man's. The men who charged her couldn't say they had offered her money for sex, so they would fabricate a story, which she would simply deny. She would become quite indignant in court, embellishing the truth and challenging the judge with her manner.

Eventually, Sarah moved into prostitution and built up a regular clientele of businessmen, whom she could phone in their cars or at their offices whenever she needed to make some money. She felt a great deal of anger towards these men, because they had something she needed. She said she hated having sex with them and was 'always acting.' She would steal from the men but they would always come back, a fact that was a great source of amusement to her.

Sarah described an approach to crime that she said many drug addicts employ in order to avoid arrest. She would do her scams for a while, then, when that became 'too hot,' she would sell cocaine; after a period of drug dealing, she would work as a prostitute, and so on.

After about three years of this life, Sarah moved to another province, where she developed a relationship with the man from whom she bought heroin. The two set up housekeeping in a 'nice apartment,' where they lived 'a pretty normal life.' He sold drugs but didn't use them, and he kept Sarah supplied with heroin. She had the time to start taking a course at school. Soon, however, they were both arrested on drug-related charges.

In the chaotic home of her childhood, Sarah was vulnerable to anyone who gave her favourable attention. Because of her charm and good looks, there was no lack of people paying attention to her, but because she had grown to distrust attention, it did not mitigate her sense of being alone. She was always wondering if other people were thinking badly of her, and she was very sensitive to criticism. Heroin eased the pain of her sensitivity and loneliness at first, but once she was addicted to the drug, she found it necessary to break the law in order to support her habit. When I asked why she had broken the law, she said, 'All I can think of is money, drugs, and because somebody else was doing it that I was with, that I loved.'

DOREEN

Doreen, a Caucasian woman, was thirty-one years old at the time of the interviews. When Doreen's feelings were hurt by someone she cared about, she would get 'mad' and slash her arms. She had deep gashes covering both arms and had had surgery four times to repair severed tendons and nerves. As a result of her slashing, she had no feeling in areas of her hands and arms. Doreen said that before she slashed, she would shake with anger; afterwards, she would feel 'relaxed.' The first time she slashed was after the CAS took her first child. She said she wouldn't go out with 'guys' because, if they saw her arms, they'd think she was 'crazy.' When she slashed, it was not her intention to kill herself; she did, however, try to commit suicide once, by swallowing three bottles of pills.

It was impossible to place details of Doreen's early life in an exact time frame. She said she remembered nothing of her childhood before the age of fourteen, but her story included details that seemed to predate that age.

Even so, her childhood memories were sparse. Although caution must be exercised in applying information from the literature to an individual case in which the individual is unable to provide a history, the fact that Doreen remembered very little from her childhood *is* consistent with the experiences of women who were sexually abused as children.[7] The other signs supporting the notion that Doreen may have been sexually abused as a child were incidents of self-mutilation and her inability to trust.[8] Moreover, Doreen was a substance abuser and had been abstinent only intermittently since the age of sixteen. Many alcoholic women and men report remembering childhood sexual abuse only after years of abstinence from alcohol or drugs.[9]

Doreen remembered enough to describe an impoverished home life with parents who were both chronic alcoholics. The house in which she grew up was cold in winter. In the morning, she and her siblings would have to stand around the stove until her mother 'got the warm morning going' – meaning that her mother would hang a blanket over the door to keep the drafts out and the heat from the stove in. Although Doreen had enough to eat and clothes to wear, her clothes weren't very nice – 'not like other people's.' Doreen went to school until she was fifteen and had completed Grade 9, although she passed Grades 7, 8, and 9 'by copying.' Her mother told her she had been 'right smart' when she was young.

Doreen recalled that her parents fought frequently and physically, and that her father, whom she described as a 'pervert' because he had a habit of sniffing her mother's underwear, severely abused her mother. Sometimes the violence was so frightening that Doreen took her siblings and ran out of the house in the hope that her father would stop.

One time I got up in the night and my mother was downstairs in the living room and she was sitting there – she was drunk and she was asleep in the chair, and she had nothing on, and she was all full of blood. And another time, my mother took me down to my aunt's place and her and my aunt went up to the bathroom. She came out of the bathroom crying ... and her legs from there to there [indicating from ankle to hip] were all black and blue.

In such a deprived, chaotic, and terrifying environment, it is remarkable that a child could survive at all. It would seem that the parents were unable to provide anything beyond the barest material essentials. Doreen was emotionally severely deprived, with the result that she craved attention and sought it wherever and from whomever she thought she could get it. In her interviews with me, she asked, several times, that I use her real name in this research so that she would be 'popular.'

Doreen started stealing her father's liquor at the age of fifteen. By six-teen, she was an alcoholic, but she 'really started drinking seriously' when, at eighteen, she moved in with her boyfriend's mother. Although she had used drugs such as hash, hash oil, cocaine, and pills, alcohol in any form, including shaving lotion, was her substance of choice and had always played a part in her conflicts with the law. During one four-month period, she drank every day and ate little; for the last two months, she couldn't get drunk and just sat in her room shaking. Doreen said she continued to drink because she always ended up in 'bad environments' when she was out of hospital or jail. Also, she felt 'smarter' when she was drunk, because she could 'talk better.' After years of excessive drinking, however, alcohol no longer made her feel better; in fact, it caused her to experience frequent blackouts. The blackouts frightened her, because it was then that she be-came 'kind of dangerous.' Once, when she was living in a halfway house, she got drunk and chased a staff member around the house with a pair of scissors. Doreen had to be told about this; she didn't remember it.

Doreen thought her brain may have been damaged from too much med-ication. She couldn't remember things: if she tried to read, then put the book down, she would forget what she had read. She said there was 'some-thing wrong' with her head, like 'there's nothing up there.' That bothered her, and she said it was the reason that she continued to drink. She pointed to a spot near her left temple and said, 'Right there, my brain feels numb.'

Doreen had given birth to three children, all of whom were adopted out. She had kept her third child for six months, an experience that made her very happy because the baby made her feel loved. It was as though the baby provided what her parents had been unable to provide. Doreen said that she used to take the baby to bed with her at night. To have the baby beside her made her feel 'good' – the same way she felt when she was with one of the two or three professional workers who, Doreen felt, cared about her.

When we met, Doreen had spent nine of the previous twelve years in one institution or another, including jails and psychiatric hospitals, where she was often restrained by a strait-jacket. She said she was 'institution-alized,' which meant that she felt safer and had a better life on the 'inside'; she wasn't able to get along well on the street.

On the 'outside,' Doreen lived on skid row; she knew which cities in two provinces had the safest parks for sleeping. She couldn't get welfare because she had no identification. Winters were usually spent in jail, al-though she spent one winter, when she was pregnant, on skid row.

Doreen found it hard to say no, and when she did have an apartment, she would take people in. As a consequence of taking in one particular man, she lost her daughter and her apartment, and ended up back on the street. The man she took in had spent more than twenty years in prison for violent crimes, and he would beat her if she refused to steal for him. One day, she stole two pairs of pants, sold one pair, and bought some wine for herself and the man. When she refused to sell the other pair because she wanted a change of clothes, he 'cracked my jaw and busted my lip and cracked my head – in front of everybody.'

Although she said she had been in trouble with the law since she was seventeen years old, Doreen was first charged by her mother when she was nineteen years old. Her mother had taken primary responsibility for the care of Doreen's first baby. One day, when Doreen was out drinking, her mother telephoned the Children's Aid Society to say that she was no longer able to care for the baby, who was ten months old by then. When Doreen discovered what had happened, she went to her mother's home and kicked the door, for which her mother had her charged. She said she and her mother had 'had problems ever since.' After her father was killed in a car accident, when Doreen was in her late teens, her mother 'kicked [her] out' of the house and forbade her to visit for many years, although she would sometimes ask her for money to pay bills. Doreen was hurt by her mother's refusal to allow her even to visit. She claimed that she was in conflict with the law because her mother wouldn't let her come home.

In both childhood and adulthood, Doreen was one of the most deprived of all the women I interviewed. In what seemed to be a hopeless life, there was still evidence that Doreen harboured hope; she had not lost her fighting spirit. And although that energy – her 'fight' – contributed to her survival, it also harmed her, because she had never been empowered to use it positively. As it was, she sometimes turned her energy against herself, particularly when she tried to cope with the hurtful actions of those she liked. At such times, she became self-destructive, attempting to relieve herself of her anger by slashing her arms.

Doreen was serving a sentence for various charges, including some related to her assaultive and threatening behaviour.

THE EMERGING PATTERN

Drug addicts are not a homogeneous group,[10] and the stories of these five women are quite different in many ways. However, a distinct pattern tracing the women's progression into drug use and conflict with the law did emerge from their stories. The pattern is interactive rather than linear, but always begins with a disconnection of some sort. The elements of the pattern are described in this section. They include disconnection, disconnection and the process of identification, the search for connection, and secondary motivation.

Disconnection

Without exception, the women in this study suffered profound and, in some cases, frequent disconnections early in their lives and throughout their lives. The disconnections took various forms, both emotional and physical. All of the women had lost, or had never had, connection with their fathers. Bonnie never knew her biological father, and her stepfather abused her physically and sexually. Margaret's father had been absent from her life for most of her first seven years, died when she was eleven, and was available in only a peripheral way in the interim. Around the age of ten, Penny lost the consistent presence of her father in her life when her parents divorced. Sarah's father was emotionally unavailable because of his alcoholism, and Doreen's father was not only an alcoholic but also a 'pervert,' who died in a car accident when she was a teenager. Four of the five women tended to idealize their fathers (in Bonnie's case, her unknown biological father) to some extent.

Along with the highly unsatisfactory or non-existent relationships with their fathers, the five women also experienced their relationships with their mothers as wanting. Although it is possible that the unsatisfactory nature of their relationships with their mothers was coincidental with their poor relationships with their fathers, it seems much more likely that the mothers were emotionally depleted and therefore unable to engage in nurturing relationships with their daughters. Some of the mothers had been severely abused by the fathers, some of the women were raised by alcoholic parents and had themselves retreated into alcoholism, and some were overburdened with children and responsibilities. Each of the five women expressed her desire to improve her connection with her mother and, as a corollary of that desire, defended at least some of her mothers' actions. At the same time, the women directed some of their anger at their mothers. Thus, unless the father had been severely abusive (as Bonnie's stepfather had been) or obviously perverted (as Doreen's father had been), he was valued. Mothers were valued but were also held responsible for the deficiencies in the women's developmental experiences.

Because of the chaotic nature of their families, the women also experienced disconnections in the relationships that would normally provide a support structure, for example, with siblings, friends, and professional people. In these cases, the siblings were usually suffering as well, and contact with school friends and sympathetic teachers was often lost because the families moved. Such relationships are important in any child's development, but they can be especially important when the primary relationships are inadequate. These women had no consistent, long-term, mutually empathic relationships. Although they had people around them, they lived in emotional isolation, a situation that Miller describes as 'destructive' and 'terrifying.'[11] Stiver conceptualizes this kind of situation as staying out of true engagement with others while giving the impression of being in relationship.[12]

Disconnection and the Process of Identification

In a relational model of development, a woman enters into a relationship of mutual identification with her mother in which each learns to respond to and care for the well-being of the other.[13] Through their empathic and reciprocal interactions, each is able to experience an affective joining while maintaining a cognitive sense of her own differentness.[14] This process of connecting and separating is essential for the emergence of 'self-boundaries,' which define where one person ends and the other begins. When children are sexually abused, they experience an invasion of their personal boundaries, and they are unable to maintain a sense of their own identity.[15] Stiver suggests that these children survive by staying out of emotional engagement,[16] a state that precludes the development of self-boundaries. It seems possible that children might be similarly affected – though perhaps less so – by other forms of abuse. Moreover, it seems that when differentiation is vague and boundaries are undefined, a daughter may experience her mother's abuse by the father as if it were her own. If a girl must be concerned for her mother's safety when her mother is being abused by the father, or if her relationship with her mother cannot be reciprocal because of mediating factors such as abuse or alcoholism, the process of identification becomes confused and disrupted. In such a relationship, the daughter may take on her mother's role in her attempts to take care of the relationship, a reversal that has been observed in other stressful situations between parents and children.[17] In the process, she is identifying with the parent in whom she perceives weaknesses, not strengths. Since, as dictated by our social structure, the father remains the more valued parent despite his abusiveness, a disconnection of the cognitive and affective states occurs with the daughter's cognitive acceptance of her father's higher value and her affective identification with her mother. When the daughter, as well as the mother, is abused by the father, the confusion of identities is reinforced. When the daughter is abused by the mother, her cognitive acceptance of her father's higher social value may be reinforced as a result of her affective disconnection from her mother, and she may attempt to identify with her father.

The Search for Connection

When serious disconnections exist within the family, the *need* for connection does not disappear. When a serious disconnection occurs, the person tries to construct an image of herself and others that will allow her to enter into relationships with the people around her.[18] In new relationships, lessons learned within the family context will therefore be repeated. When disconnection has characterized family relationships, disconnection of some sort will probably be the organizing feature in other relationships. As noted earlier, Stiver conceptualizes this situation as staying out of relationships while behaving as though in relationships.[19]

In a study of the role of peers in the etiology of drug use among female and male adolescents, it was found that the proportion of their friends who were drug users was by far the most influential factor in the adolescents' involvement with drugs.[20] Certainly, in the case of the five women discussed in this chapter, the influence of friends and family who used drugs and alcohol was a factor determining the women's initial use of those substances. Johnson, Marcos, and Bahr postulate that, 'while association with drug-using friends is certainly the key to predicting adolescent drug use, the probability of that kind of association is in turn partly a product of one's attachments and general values.'[21]

Assuming that mutually empathic relationships are important to girls' and women's psychological development, it is to be expected that if girls do not find growth-enhancing relationships within their families, they will search elsewhere for them in an attempt to meet their needs. If the objective in forming relationships is to promote growth-enhancing development, it follows that the latter would constitute the underlying motivation for seeking out relationships. Indeed, the women described in this chapter did seek out relationships, but those relationships were not growth-promoting. Instead, they were often organized around an intermediary element – drugs or alcohol – and in many ways mimicked the relationships for which the women were attempting to compensate. The use of drugs or alcohol gave the 'illusion of connection' while the women continued to be shut off from relationships in which they could relate authentically.[22]

Brown elaborates on the concept of alcohol as a central organizing principle in families of alcoholics. A fundamental component of families that are organized around alcohol is denial of the existence of alcoholism, and since the family is invested in the denial of reality, the result is a disconnection of the family members from one another.[23] Brown's description of the role alcohol plays as a central organizing principle applies equally well to the kinds of relationships in which the women became involved as a result of their search for connection. Lacking the experience of empathic connecting, their search led them to the spurious safety of the familiar – that is, relationships in which the other person was unresponsive. Often, the lack of responsiveness was a product of drug or alcohol abuse.

Another facet of the search for connection is related to the powerful influence of siblings in a family in which the parents are not responsive to the needs of their children. Sarah, for example, was introduced to lawbreaking by her brother Jason, an impressive character who gave her the attention she craved. At the age of nine, when he was soliciting her help with his heists, she was unable to understand that the attention he gave her was to satisfy his own purposes. None the less, Jason may have inadvertently mediated a connection between Sarah and her mother. Sarah remarked that she always accompanied her mother on visits to Jason when he was in custody. Because it was always Sarah and her mother and no other family members who made the visits, she may have felt a certain collegiality with her mother at those times that she may have interpreted as responsiveness on her mother's part.

Secondary Motivation

In their search for connection, the women fell into relationships in which drugs and/or alcohol featured prominently. The use of drugs, in particular, held great appeal for the women. It provided them with a reason for spending time with particular others who provided distraction and may have produced a sense of normalcy for the women and, thus, a feeling of belonging in the world. Bonnie was fascinated by the 'weird' people who bought or tried to buy her services, and Margaret became preoccupied with 'helping' addicts who she believed were far more hopelessly addicted than she was.

Through the rituals it involves, drug use provided the women with a superficial connection to others. In addition, it substantially, if temporarily, reduced the emotional pain they experienced as a result of disconnection. Substance abuse became the focal point of the women's lives, and illegal activities were often pursued in its service. For Sarah and Penny, who were addicted to heroin, the threat of the physical pain of withdrawal provided a particular kind of secondary motivation for lawbreaking. They knew that, if they failed to obtain a supply of heroin, they would soon lapse into withdrawal. Through their addiction, they were distracted from their emotional pain; it was far easier to focus on and try to manage the physical pain of withdrawal.

With the reinforcement of these secondary sources of motivation, the women became embroiled in lives of drug and alcohol use, and lawbreaking to support their addictions.

FROM DISCONNECTION TO LAWBREAKING

Central to the lawbreaking experiences of these women was their disconnection, on two levels, from responsive others. First, they endured disconnections from important people in their lives (in some cases, in the most extreme forms, such as death or abandonment), and some experienced the loss of self-boundaries as a result of sexual or physical abuse, or both. Second, they were left to fend for themselves in the face of those disconnections. In their attempts to find responsive others, they became involved in drug and alcohol abuse. Although drug dependency has no single cause for these women, disconnection was an important precursor. There is reason to suspect that losses experienced early in life, especially when bereft children have inadequate emotional support, can have dramatic effects. If a person has to deal with death issues early in life, pathology may develop.[24]

No attempt was made in this study to detect particular pathologies or to label family pathology. Observations have been limited to descriptive accounts of the events that the participants felt were important in the chronicle of their lives. However, the events they described, along with their reactions to those events, were consistent with the idea that disconnections from important others, in the absence of relationships with others who are responsive to their experiences, can have serious repercussions. For the women discussed in this chapter, the path eventually led to conflict with the law.

5

The Women's Words: Visible Anger

Anger was the catalyst for the activities that brought Vicki, Doris, and Danielle into conflict with the law. For both Vicki and Doris, anger became their primary mode of expression when other emotions became too overwhelming or could not be expressed. Danielle's anger grew out of repeated violations of trust and repeated abuse.

At nineteen, Vicki was the youngest participant in the research. She was an Aboriginal Canadian, raised on a reserve, and her native language was her first language.

Vicki was raised by her maternal grandparents. Her mother worked in a city in the 'south,' and sent money for her; she never got support from her father and had met him only a few times. Her mother visited sometimes, and Vicki felt happy when she came, but when she left again, Vicki 'couldn't stand it no more.'

Vicki's grandmother raised six grandchildren as well as her own ten children. When she was very young, Vicki had been taken for a while by the Children's Aid Society, but she couldn't remember living with anyone but her grandparents. Her grandparents supported themselves with a cheque 'coming from somewhere.' When all the bills were paid, they'd use the leftover money to buy 'booze' or to play bingo. When her grandparents were drinking, her cousins would look after her, or she and her cousins would look after each other. She would tell her grandparents when she had problems, and they would give her advice; she usually tried to do what they wanted. She spent her days on the reserve sitting and walking around and cleaning her grandparents' house. Vicki said it didn't bother

her that she had nothing to do, because that's the way it was on the reserve. Vicki completed Grade 8.

The reserve was a dangerous place. When they were drinking, people would 'fight and almost kill each other'; some were shot or stabbed. Teenagers would start drinking and 'go into people's houses and bust windows.' When they stopped drinking, the people would 'regret' what they'd done. Vicki herself had been fighting since she was young; she fought with a lot of people. Vicki started using drugs (hash) when she was fourteen. She tried sniffing gasoline, but quit when her best friend died in a fire that started when she (the friend) was sniffing. She also began drinking at a very early age – she couldn't remember when – but her drinking didn't concern her. She 'just thought [worried] about [her] trouble-making.'

Vicki said she had 'lost too many people.' In addition to her best friend, she had lost one of her brothers, who was murdered when he was a baby, before she was born, and her paternal grandparents, who died when she was a child. Even though she really didn't know the latter three, their deaths hurt her, because 'it was too late to get to know them.' She'd also lost an aunt who overdosed when Vicki was sixteen, and an uncle who shot himself in the kitchen of the house in which she lived when she was eight. Vicki had been told a few hours before the aunt overdosed that she was going to do it, but she didn't believe it. Her family later said, 'It's OK . . . nobody can live that long – can't live forever.' (Her aunt was in her thirties and had six children).

Vicki said, 'I can't take it no more; I have to get used to it ... losing people and all that – I have to get used to it, get them out of my mind before it's too late. I might lose my memory or something.'

Vicki went to jail for setting a fire on the reserve where she lived. She had done it, she said, 'to get that anger out of my system.' Vicki had told her grandmother on the day of the incident that she wanted to go into the city to stay with her mother for a while, as she had done before. Her grandmother's response to her suggestion was unexpected; she said that if Vicki went to see her mother, she should not return to the reserve; she should stay in the city and find a job. Vicki said she was 'pissed off' that her grandmother would say such a thing to her. She thought that her grandmother was afraid she would abandon her and her grandfather.

It really hurt though – after she told me that. I didn't like it the way she told that, 'cause they know I love them and I know they love me.

Vicki's initial response to her grandmother's ultimatum was not anger.

Rather, she was 'depressed' by her grandmother's reaction, but she wasn't able to admit her true feelings to her grandmother.

I was just feeling depressed after she told me that, and I just kept it in me – inside of me all this time – inside my system – I just kept it all down ever since she told me that.

If Vicki had been able to express her feelings to her grandmother, she might have been able to achieve at least some resolution of both her feelings and the situation. However, to admit that one can be hurt by another's comments is to admit caring about that person, and, although Vicki knew that she loved her grandparents and that they loved her, she had never been able to tell them so face to face.

I couldn't tell them in front of them, face to face, 'cause sometimes many people are shy to say something. 'Cause I'm not used to it – saying something like 'I love you.'

According to Vicki, she and many others on the reserve were unaccustomed to expressing strong positive feelings for others. She said they cried with grief when someone died, and they fought on one another's behalf with outsiders such as the police, but to admit that they cared about someone – even a loved grandparent – meant risking vulnerability in a place where it did not feel safe to be vulnerable. In the volatile milieu of the reserve, 'softer' feelings were lost. Judging from Vicki's comments, people on the reserve touched one another emotionally and physically in crisis and in anger, not in verbal expressions of love. In addition, Vicki felt uncomfortable expressing her true feelings because of the lack of privacy on the reserve.

I can't talk to anybody else about this, like on the reserve, 'cause once I talk about it, they're going all over it, and everybody on the reserve is going to hear what I said.

Moreover, she could not retreat to privacy even in her own home, where she might have been able to calm herself down, because her grandmother would follow her into her room.

I couldn't 'cause they're in the same place ... I couldn't lock myself in the room because we don't have no locks on those doors.

What, then, does a person do when she has strong feelings she wishes to express or manage, but is powerless to do so? Caplan writes that anger can help to overcome feelings of powerlessness. She points out that

Anger is a secondary emotion. We don't go from feeling nothing to feeling angry. Anger is usually the feeling we have when we don't like having an earlier feeling.[1]

Acting in a manner consistent with this notion of anger as a secondary emotion, Vicki focused not on her hurt and depression but on being 'pissed off' over the unfortunate interaction between her and her grandmother. Tavris suggests that anger is used to make a grievance known.[2] Indeed, Vicki let her depression be known through the vehicle of anger. Living on a reserve in which people regularly acted out their anger, Vicki had a sort of cultural affirmation and paradigm for this method of dealing with her original feelings. It was usual, even expected – in the sense that it happened regularly – for people on the reserve to fight to 'get rid' of their anger. Thus, violence was common behaviour on the reserve.

People over there, they fight each other. They almost kill each other. They end up in the hospital. I know people getting shot ... people getting stabbed. It's dangerous over there to live 'cause in the nighttime when teenagers start drinking, they could come to your house and start busting windows.

Anger was acted out violently under the influence of alcohol. 'They do that only when they drink. They don't do that when they don't drink.' Certainly, physical fighting was a mode of expression with which Vicki was very familiar. She started fighting when she was young – so young, that she was unable to remember the first time she'd fought. Moreover, she said that beating someone up was the only way she knew to deal with anger.

Although in her milieu Vicki was restricted to the expression of only certain feelings – particularly anger – and had learned to express those feelings through fighting, she was not always comfortable with that mode of expression. With respect to the incident with her grandmother, she felt that it was wrong to fight with her because her grandmother was too old. In past arguments with her, when she was conflicted about fighting her physically, she would instead fight anyone who was supporting her grandmother in the argument. However, she felt that such action was unfair.

Not going to go pick on somebody else just because my grandparents told me not to come back home ... I don't like to go picking on somebody else while I have problems with my grandparents.

In addition, because of the many losses of family that Vicki had already experienced in her lifetime and the regrets that accompanied those losses, she knew that she would ultimately regret getting angry with her grandparents. She said, 'after I get angry I feel sorry for them after [sic] 'cause I know I'm going to regret it after I lose them.' None the less, she was experiencing her depression as anger, and she had a limited repertoire of skills for dealing with anger. Moreover, she could not count on her elders to set limits on her behaviour.

Her practical training for participation in the violence she observed on the reserve began early in life. It was common practice for teenagers to act destructively on the reserve, and her induction into the 'typical' teenage role of violator involved an encounter with the law at the age of twelve.

One night when she was out with two girlfriends, three boys approached them and said they were going to do a 'b & e' – a break and enter. The girls decided to go along for 'something to do.' Vicki said that such activities were common for young people on the reserve, who 'get excited' and 'want to do something to get themselves into trouble.' She and her friends 'just went inside the store and started taking stuff.' Vicki 'didn't think about it,' she 'just did it.' They were caught the next day, and she was given a suspended sentence.

Between the ages of twelve and sixteen, Vicki continued to do 'b & e's,' was 'on probation all the time,' and was incarcerated for several months as a young offender. When she was sixteen, she tried unsuccessfully to stop these activities. 'You know how kids are when they get carried away easily – they get so excited and they won't stop ... I couldn't quit till now.'

Although she thought that her behaviour was commonplace, Vicki believed that her grandparents were not in favour of what she was doing.

Vicki's grandparents were unable to set limits on her behaviour. When she participated in her first 'b & e,' her grandfather's sister happened to be visiting, and according to Vicki, they couldn't punish her, because the sister might think they always punished her; in fact, they 'never' punished her for anything. Vicki thought that if they had punished her, she might have avoided jail later, because she would have known 'what punishment feels like' and would have been less likely to incur it again.

Although it is doubtful that Vicki really wanted severe corporal (or other) punishment, she seemed to feel she needed to be taught the boundaries of acceptable behaviour. As Tavris points out in her discussion of the ways in which various cultures deal with anger, setting such limits is no more than what is a designated task of friends, relatives, and tribes the world over – to pass along rules for controlling anger.[3]

In all likelihood, the burden of their large family, combined with their drinking, reduced the grandparents' effectiveness in the parental role. In addition, they may have been influenced and constrained by the conventions of the reserve, and powerless in face of the social influences that prevailed there. Whatever the reason, it seems that, in the absence of early limit-setting, Vicki eventually became too difficult for her grandparents to handle.

They couldn't say anything to me 'cause they know how I am. Like when they piss me off – they usually don't piss me off no more 'cause they know how I am, how I lose my temper easy.

Vicki's solution to her dilemma with her grandmother was to devise a plan to release her anger: she would set a fire. She announced her intention to an uncle and her grandfather, who, she felt, did not believe her. (Or, perhaps, given her unmanageability, they felt powerless to stop her.) That night, she set fire to an abandoned building.

I couldn't do anything else to get it [the anger] out ... besides arson, I could've just went out and probably pick on anybody and start beating her up or him.

Although Vicki did not succeed in managing her anger in a nondestructive way, she did choose to set fire to an *abandoned* building. Clearly, she sought to find some sort of resolution to her feelings, not to hurt someone.

Bernardez writes that 'frequently the reason why certain angry reactions are of inappropriate intensity is that they are repetitions of unexpressed frustrations in the past.'[4] She had been abandoned by her mother and was being threatened with the loss of the only caregivers she had known. She was torn between the people she loved most, and was threatened once again with disconnection. Her immediate emotional responses were hurt and depression, but because she had no vehicles for the expression and management of those feelings, she expressed them through anger, a customary mode of expression in her cultural milieu.

Strickly speaking, Vicki's feelings about having been abandoned by her mother were not entirely unexpressed. In fact, she believed that her problems were a result of her upbringing on the reserve, and that, if she had been 'taken [from the hospital, as a baby, by someone other than her grandparents, someone who did not live on the reserve] to the States or somewhere,' she would have had a better life. Since her mother made her home in a city, the thought of being abandoned to life on the reserve must have been especially painful for Vicki. Much as she loved her grandparents, the very fact that they had raised her on the reserve, which she believed to be the source of her problems, was probably a contributing factor to the tension in the relationship.

Although she did not raise the issue specifically, it is possible that Vicki also felt some guilt about her desire to spend time with her mother. Ultimately, by acting as she did, she temporarily escaped the pressure involved in making a choice between the people she loved.

In Vicki's comment about the possibility of a better life elsewhere, she seemed to imply that it would be a mistake to think that her anger was an expression only of the frustrations in her interactions with her family. All around her, people were acting out in violence. She witnessed violence almost routinely on the reserve, a situation that has also been described by other female Aboriginal lawbreakers.[5] She had seen her grandfather fight, and had stood by, as a child, watching an aunt die of a drug overdose, and an uncle die of a self-inflicted gunshot wound. LaPrairie notes that 'observers of the high levels of violence in some Indian communities have suggested that internalized oppression and alienation cause people to turn to violence.'[6] The intermediate step between oppression and alienation, on the one hand, and violence, on the other, would be anger.

Although she did have some awareness of the origin of Aboriginal people's oppression, her anger remained focused on immediate issues and had not yet been politicized. All around her, she saw the violence, separation, and pain that had grown out of her people's history of oppression, but she had not yet linked those horrors to her mother's abandonment of her or to her upbringing in an environment in which there was no possibility that her needs would be met. Therefore, she was unable to channel her anger into productive activity; she was able only to act on current events within her personal domain.

The plight of Aboriginal Canadians is well known. Descriptions of their lives reveal people who are struggling to maintain their culture and retrieve the values and dignity that, for many, have been lost.[7] The tension between the alienation and oppression identified by LaPrairie and the struggle to be free of those constraints affects all who must live in such an environment.[8] In such a tension-filled milieu, it is not surprising that misunderstandings occur between generations or that stories like Vicki's are one outcome.

DORIS

Doris, a forty-eight-year-old Caucasian woman, suffered from disabling arthritis. When she was only two months old, her parents were killed in a car crash. She said her birth was not registered anywhere, and she joked about her origins, saying, 'I come from another planet.' After the accident, she was sent to live with a family in which there were six other children. Doris's foster father was an alcoholic who 'drank' all of the family's money. The family survived on relief, so food was scarce, the house was cold, and family members slept three to a bed.

Doris said she'd been in trouble with the law since she was three years old. By that time, her foster mother couldn't handle her; still in diapers, Doris would run away to the next-door neighbour for warm milk for her bottle. She said that, during their early childhood, she often stayed away from the foster home, stealing meat and cheese from a store as well as clothes from the neighbours' clothes-lines, hiding in woodsheds, and sleeping under porches and in box cars, where she would 'burrow into a hole in the sawdust like a little beaver.' She said, 'It's a wonder I never froze to death.' She remembered that she had been beaten by both foster parents, but that they never reported her missing during her absences.

At the age of seven, Doris had been in school only six months when she was hit by a truck that had gone out of control. She spent almost two years recovering in hospital. During this period, her foster mother died. Doris was taken in a wheelchair to the cemetery, where she attempted to 'roll into the grave' to be with her foster mother, the only person to whom she had ever felt any closeness. Long-term hospitalization in a psychiatric facility followed her recuperation at the age of nine.

Doris was first married at the age of twelve. Before she began to menstruate, she had sex with a thirty-two-year-old janitor in the hospital where she was staying. Doctors labelled the act rape because her blouse was torn, but Doris said she had 'wanted it,' and that she used to walk along the hospital corridors 'smooching' with the man. The parents of the man felt disgraced and forced a marriage, whereupon Doris went to live with the family. Doris gave birth to a son; a few weeks later, her husband died in an accident. Doris had a 'nervous breakdown' and was readmitted to hospital. The baby was left with his grandparents, and Doris said he died, although later she admitted he was 'dead' only to her.

Doris said that, during the following period of hospitalization, she was whipped with an 'electric whip.' She said that some people died from similar whippings and were buried on hospital grounds. A woman related to Doris's first husband noticed Doris's wounds when she had her out of the hospital on a day pass. The woman took her to a physician, who lodged a complaint, initiating an investigation that, according to Doris, eventually resulted in the closing of the hospital.

Doris was moved to another hospital at the age of eighteen and stayed there until she was twenty-four. During this period, she was on several types of medication – dilantin, phenobarbital, and largactyl. She also began to abuse alcohol.

When Doris was discharged from hospital, she went to live with her foster grandmother, whom Doris described as a very strict woman. The period between her final discharge from hospital and the time of our interviews was characterized by change and upheaval. She said she married another six times, searching for the love and care she needed, but divorced each time. It was typical of the men in her life to leave in the morning and never return.

For many years, alcohol played a central role in Doris's life. She would frequently meet men in bars, and would go to their rooms on the promise of 'a bottle'; she said she wanted both the drink and the sex that inevitably followed. Although she denied being a prostitute on the grounds that she never charged for sex, the men usually left money for her. Doris's only friends were people she met in bars, and when she swore off alcohol one day about a year before the birth of her last child, she gave up her friends too.

Doris said she'd had twelve children, but she didn't count her oldest son, who was 'dead' to her. There had been some multiple births and several deaths, and Doris said that five children were still living. All the children had been taken by the Children's Aid Society, with the exception of the youngest, who had been raised by Doris and was being cared for by a friend during her incarceration.

Money was usually in short supply, and for some time Doris lived in a rural area, where she hunted for her food. Police made numerous trips to her home to 'bug her' about her guns; a scuffle would break out occasionally, and Doris would be charged. Although she was charged many times, she was usually only fined or sentenced to a day in jail.

Like Vicki, Doris was serving a sentence for setting a fire, but she claimed to be innocent of the charge. She said that the fire was really her husband's doing, but that the police believed her husband was innocent because he didn't have a police record. She, however, had an extensive record, consisting mostly of charges for assault and public mischief.

I admit that I had misgivings about parts of Doris's story. Confronted with the prospect that some details of her story might be the product of imagination, or confabulation, rather than reality, and wanting to believe her but also wanting to be rigorous in conducting the research, I decided that in trying to understand her conflicts with the law I would rely primarily on my interactions with her, my reactions to her, and her statements pertaining to her feelings about her life. I was also aware, however, that what may seem to be truly incredible occurrences really do happen to people – perhaps to women, in particular – and that Doris's appearance, lack of education, and emotionality might cast doubt where none should exist. Therefore, I incorporated her contribution to the study by examining my reactions to her and the content of her story, being particularly critical of my reactions to her.

Without question, Doris had been arrested on many occasions and had served at least one previous sentence in prison. Judging from what I observed of her in the institution and by the reactions of staff and other inmates to her, I believed it was possible that at least some of the charges she had faced in the past were the result of hostile interactions with the police more than of anything else she might have done. It was certain, however, that Doris had been, and continued to be, assaultive. I witnessed some of her angry exchanges with other inmates and correctional officers, and she told me about an incident that had occurred the last time she was in prison, in which she assaulted another inmate.

I had no doubt that Doris was an angry woman. When I asked her if she felt she was an angry person, she replied, 'Yes and no. If I'm left alone, no, but if they don't leave me alone, I have to get angry.' Her choice, then, seemed to be that she could be alone or she could be angry. She said she felt 'angry inside ... quite a bit,' and that, on the 'outside' (that is, outside prison), she did not feel angry because she did not come into contact with many people. She claimed that when she did encounter people on the outside, 'we know how to talk to each other.' It was evident from other statements she made that most of her associations outside prison were with staff members of various social services agencies, and if she had contact only with people who could be counted on to help her, she tended not to be assaultive.

The best method of assessing the way Doris came into conflict with the law was simply to observe her. She felt that she had never been loved and that she had become unlovable; she had never been taught to manage her reactions and so was aggressive when emotionally hurt in even the slightest way. She said, 'I don't take any bullshit from anybody,' and she admitted that she said 'things that shouldn't be said' in order to control both the other inmates and the anger she felt inside. She described her verbal abuse of others as the result of a choice between hitting and yelling at them. She felt she had to fight for her very survival. 'I was a fighter; I wanted to fight for everything I got. I always had to fight my own battles.'

Doris had spent a lifetime living by her wits. She felt that her assaultive tendencies were a result of the mistreatment she had received when she was growing up, and she also knew that she could use those tendencies to garner attention and have her physical needs met. She remembered that, when she was in hospital, between the ages of seven and nine, she would hit out at the nurses to get their attention. If the hospital staff brought her meal tray later than she had expected it, she would throw the tray across the room. As an adult, she threatened or assaulted people, and in prison, she swore and shook her fist at people in order to get her way. For her, anger and fighting were synonymous. She said she would put up with so much, and then, when she couldn't take it any more, she would strike. Her anger and fighting were vehicles for getting what she needed. Tavris suggests that anger survives as a response when it works.[9] It seems that anger worked for Doris at least some of the time, to the extent that it made her feel she had some control over events and situations that she found threatening.

None the less, as Doris discovered, anger and fighting are not without their price. By the time she was grown, she felt that nobody wanted her, but she had become resigned to her way of life. She said that she had always survived by fighting and that that was the way it would always be. 'I was raised to be rough and tough, and I will always be rough and tough.' Her battle was a hard and lonely one. 'I fight my own battles. It takes strength. I'm trying to keep the strength. It's hard.'

As my interviews with Doris progressed, I was always aware of an underlying sadness and vulnerability. She said that she was treated as though she didn't exist in the prison, protesting, 'I exist, I'm human, and I have feelings.' At times, those feelings were overwhelming. 'Sometimes I feel I'm a burden on people; I wish I weren't existing because then people would leave me alone.' Such a profoundly joyless statement is suggestive of great pain and sadness, which Doris could tolerate and survive only by redirecting her focus to anger.

Not surprisingly, in my interactions with Doris, I found that she was slow to trust and always wary, even though she wanted to trust. When she felt safe, she responded with childlike delight. Each of my meetings with her began with a small test for me. It seemed that she was trying to determine whether I would continue to be supportive of her and show kindness and understanding, or whether I, too, would desert her emotionally. It was clear that, if I disappointed her, she would become angry in order to fend off the familiar pain of loss.

Although she defended her method of survival, Doris had regrets about her life. 'I had to fight to survive the way I did, but what did it get me? It put me in here.' Doris believed that if she'd had parents to love her, 'none of this would have happened.' She said, 'If children aren't raised the right way, they can't do anything but break the law. If you're five years old and not cared for, you steal food.' She felt that, at her age, she was beyond help and that 'they' should have started when she was about fourteen 'to make something decent out of me. If somebody would have loved me and cared for me, it would have helped – even as a teenager.' Doris felt that she was 'still a kid' in the sense that she needed a lot of caring. She felt she was a 'burden' on people and wished she didn't exist; it was only her son that kept her alive.

For Doris, anger grew out of deprivation, rejection, and abandonment; of being the recipient of care within systems that were responsible for her but ill-equipped to provide a real home; and of the feelings that accompanied all these experiences. Doris's anger had been sustained for most of her life; it manifested itself in her fighting approach to life, which, when she was young, had been essential to her survival. As she grew older, her anger kept people at a distance or propelled her into conflict with others. However, she desperately desired contact with people from whom she could receive the nurturing she knew she needed. Perhaps the anger was simply less painful than the sadness, loneliness, and extreme deprivation she felt.

DANIELLE

The seeds of Danielle's anger were sown early in her life. Danielle, age thirty-three, was raised on a farm as an only child. Her parents had another child, but she was sixteen years old when Danielle arrived, and she left home to be married when Danielle was quite young. With no children for playmates and only her pets as confidants, Danielle described her early childhood as 'boring' and 'lonely.' Her parents were emotionally undemonstrative and inaccessible, old-fashioned in their ideas about raising children, and strict; she knew they cared for her only because they provided sufficiently for her material needs. They met her material needs so well that she stood out among the children at school, who were not as well dressed as she was and who did not bring treats to school in their lunches as she did – although they did sometimes have spending money, which Danielle never had, because her parents were 'cheap.'

Danielle's primary activity on the farm was 'work, work, work,' which she normally did alongside her father, in the barn, on the tractor, or in the fields. Although she was proud of her work on the farm and enjoyed the animals, she regretted that her mother, who preferred to work alone in the kitchen, never taught her to cook.

Danielle thought of her father as a great man who 'hates all evil things,' which, to his mind, included alcohol, cigarettes, and drugs. Danielle's mother was the disciplinarian, punishing Danielle by making her sit and read French books from school. Danielle didn't remember being spanked, and she never saw her parents angry, but neither did she remember kisses, hugs, affection, or sympathy. Ever since childhood, she disliked being touched, and she touched her own children only because she felt she should.

Until she was ten years old, school was lonely but bearable. Then, she learned that she had been adopted at the age of two months.

And it wasn't from my parents either. It was from school ... some girls told me on the bus. I was going back home and – I guess their parents were talking and they heard that – and they started to call me son of a bitch – well daughter of a bitch.

Danielle was hurt, humiliated, and frightened, but she was unable to express her feelings to her parents. Instead, she reacted with anger, which she took out on them.

I was crying – my mom and dad was wondering, 'What's wrong with you' – and I started screaming, packed up my little suitcase, and I said 'I'm going to look for my mom. That's it. You're not my parents. You don't tell me what to do.' From that day on, the rebel inside of me always went against them because I was saying 'Well, you're not my parents, you're not gonna tell me what to do.'

Danielle said, 'When I learned that I was adopted, that's when it changed a lot of things.' Danielle was jarred into a sense of insecurity by the news of her adoption. She also began to feel that the people she knew as her aunts and uncles treated her differently from the way they treated her parents' biological daughter, which made Danielle feel that she was not related to them. She felt that she no longer belonged with the people she had always known as her family. At the same time, the news of her adoption rang true: It was consistent with her sense of separateness from her parents, which was a product of their emotional distance from her.

Once the news was out, life at school became intolerable, increasing her sense of isolation. Every day was 'another day in hell.' The other children teased her and were abusive; they once buried her in a snowbank, leaving her there for two hours. The nuns who taught at the school were unsympathetic – they were even abusive themselves – and they did not attempt to stop the children's ill treatment of her. Danielle said that one nun told her, 'You don't belong here. You are an adopted child. It's a sin.'

I was angry at the nuns. Oh boy, yes, I was very, very angry at the nuns. Yeh, I would swear at them in French, oh boy! They should've treated me with respect, to tell the other kids to leave me alone ... Don't have to give me the strap. I don't know why they even bothered to give me the strap, because I didn't even do nothing; it was the other kids that were after my hide, not the other way around, so that one I could never figure out.

Danielle was affected in profound ways by these events.

Because of all this, in school I used to pee myself ... pee in class and everybody would be laughing their guts out because it would be all wet. *I* would be all wet. Even the teacher, the nun, would laugh at me.

Danielle was greatly distressed and angered by the abuse she experienced at the hands of the other children and the nuns. She began to learn to cope with her feelings by blocking them out, 'because other than that, I would be angry all the time.' With the added components of her loneliness and humiliation, as well as her need to feel a permanent connection to someone – to find a place where she belonged – the stage was set for the developments that followed.

In the 'lonely, lonely life' that Danielle led, she had only her cat and her dog for comfort. She had a tree house in the bush on the farm, and she would go there with her cat and dog to cry, asking them why she didn't have any friends at school.

When she was thirteen years old, Danielle fell in love with Sandy, a seventeen-year-old who was working on the neighbouring farm. Taking advantage of Danielle's need to be loved, Sandy coerced her into having sex with him.

... when I first met him [...] he was sexually abusive – was making love suppos-edly. I was crying. I was crying through the whole thing. And Sandy says, 'That's it,' he says, 'I'm never gonna make love to you again.' And I'm going, 'That's fine with me. I don't like it anyways.' We didn't see each other for about three weeks and I cried, 'Oh no! What did I do?' So from then on I kept on making love all the time because I didn't want to lose him, that's why.

Sandy continued to threaten to leave her if she refused to have sex with him. 'He was saying that if I didn't do it he would leave me, so I loved him so much – I adored the man.'

When she was seventeen, they ran away together, Danielle became preg-nant, and they returned to their home town to be married. Danielle's parents were vehemently opposed to Sandy and had always made it dif-ficult for her to date him. She felt that part of her reason for getting married was that she 'wanted to get out of the house.' She gave birth to a daughter, Sophie, and, a year later, to a son, Jean. It was after Jean was born that Sandy became violent. Jean was much slower developmentally than Sophie, and Sandy blamed Danielle. 'For some reason he always said, "Oh, it's all your fault, you're the one who carried the fucking thing." ' Danielle always tried to defend Jean and, as a result, often found herself on the receiving end of Sandy's anger. Sometimes he beat her, and some-times he threw her and the children out of the house and forced them to spend the night outside in the cold. On one occasion, Sandy put the barrel of a gun in Jean's mouth because the boy refused to eat his oatmeal. On another occasion, Sandy lost his temper because Jean had defecated in his pants, when Sandy thought he should already have been toilet-trained. Danielle tried unsuccessfully to get to Jean to change him before Sandy noticed.

He got up and pushed me out of the way. I had a bag of groceries and the bag flew, and he goes, 'You little son of a bitch, you shit in your fucking pants.' He says, 'I'll teach you where to shit' and then all hell broke loose. And my husband took the shit out of – the thing, put it in the toilet, mixed it with the water and then took my son and says, 'There, that's where you fucking shit if you wanna shit.' So I took the baseball bat and – smack – 'You leave him alone, you leave him alone.' And he says 'You fucking bitch, you're never gonna get me again,' so I got one hell of a beating. Was a week in the hospital from that one ... Had my jaw broken, my two ribs broken, couldn't walk, I was black and blue because when he punched me, I flew through the patio door ... Jean was screaming, Sophie too, 'Leave mom alone, leave mom alone.' Well, Jean took a fork and tried to stab his father ... Oh man, did he fly. Sandy took him by the arm and made him fly from one end to the other end of the lawn.

Danielle tried to press charges on that occasion and many more (seventy-six times, in total), but her efforts were fruitless. She claimed that the police refused to pursue the matter of her and her children's abuse because it fell into the category of 'domestic violence.' Danielle was extremely angry at the police and felt that, if she had been a drinker during her marriage to Sandy, her fate might have been a much longer jail term, because, under the influence of alcohol, she probably would have killed him.

Eventually, despite the fact that she had no financial resources, Danielle could take the abuse no longer and decided to leave. 'I just woke up one morning and that was it. I packed the bags and the children and said, "Let's go." ' Although she had made a courageous move, Danielle felt that she had lost a great deal by leaving her husband, and her notion of herself as a 'loser' was reinforced.

Danielle supported her children on social assistance for about a year. Then she met Peter, the father of her third child. For the first three years, he was 'a darn good man and a good father. Yeh, a very nice man at first. But he lost his arm in a mill accident.' Peter experienced severe pain with the loss of his arm, and since he did not like to take pills, he began to drink.

So he started to drink, and he was fun at first. I laughed at his drinking, but then it was not funny anymore. He started to get very jealous, possessive. I couldn't even go to my mother or father and he started to be very violent. I called Peter 'the axeman,' because, when he was drunk, he used to go around me with an axe. Tried to cut me on my head. He missed, a lot, but the furniture he didn't miss. The fridge was all smashed, the table ... oh what a mess!

The situation with Peter was very distressing. Danielle had trusted him because he had never hit her when he was sober, and, for three years, she had found him to be a good partner and father. Despite the abuse that began after he lost his arm, she stayed with him for another three years. Moreover, she learned from Sandy and Peter that it was not wise to fight back.

What's the use? They get twice, three times as mad, you get four times as much beat up. No, I just got tired of getting beat up. That's all; because the more I would try and defend myself, the more shit I would get kicked out of me.

After six years with Peter, Danielle found herself on her own again, this time with three children. Once again, she relied on welfare for her income, but the situation was complicated by the lack of housing in her area. Finally, she found a place, but it had 'no water, no hydro, and it was snowing in the house.'

She met Marc, who rescued her and the children. He bought a house for them and treated them well. 'At first I was so happy being there, and then . . . I didn't feel like I belonged there and things went worse because I started drinking.' She had internalized the abuse she had experienced at the hands of others – school children, nuns, men – and had begun to feel that she deserved to be abused. Accordingly, she started to abuse herself. 'I would hurt myself, punch windows out, just cut myself and bang myself and put my hand right through the wall.' When she drank, she would call herself names – a 'fucking bitch,' 'useless,' 'no good,' an 'incompetent mother,' a 'nobody,' a 'loser.'

Her abysmal perception of herself was reinforced when she and Sophie were involved in a car accident in which Sophie's face was scarred. Danielle had been drinking and had asked someone else to drive Marc's car. Even though she wasn't driving, Danielle blamed herself for Sophie's injuries because she had insisted that Sophie accompany her. She was also angry at herself because Marc's new car had been badly damaged. In the end, Danielle was so disgusted with herself that she began drinking heavily to 'punish' herself.

Danielle's story was similar to the stories of both Vicki and Doris, in that her anger was an outgrowth of her feelings of vulnerability. Judging from the accounts of such researchers as Browne[10] and Walker,[11] her story climaxed, with her assault on Marc, in a manner similar to that of other women who seriously assault or kill their partners.

I was drinking at the time and I used a knife on the man that I was living with because I was fed up with getting beat up ... I was just fed up with men taking me as a punching bag and this time I used a weapon instead of my hands ... almost killed the man too.

Danielle saw her anger as a product of time and events.

... so my anger was getting built up. It wasn't all complete in one day ... I got so many [beatings] from Sandy and Peter that they build me up so much anger towards men that, even some girls [in the prison] will talk about 'Oh, well, I deserved it.' Oh my, I'm telling you, my face turns purple and I start sweating because I get so mad when a woman says she deserved to get hit. I really get – oh, it just gets me because nobody, I don't care if you're the worst bitch in the world, no woman deserves to get hit by a man.

Marc was Danielle's third partner and the man who, she felt, least deserved her attack. He was the 'best man' she had ever been with, but he became the target for her anger because of her underlying fear and her determination that she would not be victimized again.

Despite her negative self-image, Danielle had retained enough self-respect to extract a promise from Marc that he would never hit her, and he kept his promise. However, on the day that she stabbed him, they had both drunk to excess and had started to throw objects. When Danielle threw Marc's stereo, he grabbed her hair. With that, Danielle lost control, thinking that the old cycle of abuse was about to be repeated.

That day he was very drunk, very upset with me, and he pulled my hair. And to me, in my mind – maybe if I would not have been drunk I would've known, but – well, none of this woulda happened anyways, but because I was drunk I became very, very angry. I said 'Here we go.' It seems like everything from the past came back and I said 'Never, never, you're not going to touch me no more.' I became purple, like ... My kids say my eyes rolled because I was that upset, I was that mad. I said, 'No way ...' 'cause maybe – maybe in my mind I thought if he pulls my hair maybe next time, punch me.

Determined that she would not be subjected to such abuse in another relationship, Danielle, in her rage, defended herself. When her children tried to intervene, she pushed them away, grabbed a butcher knife, and 'went berserk.'

Throughout her life, Danielle was traumatized by shock, disappointments, and abuse. When she was informed, in a cruel manner and not by her family, that she had been adopted, she was undoubtedly confused. As the daughter of parents who were not demonstrative or inclined to verbalize reassurances of their support, she already felt isolated and very lonely. There was no one with whom she could share her feelings, and suddenly she discovered that even her relationship with her emotionally distant parents was not what she had believed it to be. Perhaps the news explained her parents' aloofness, perhaps she suddenly felt that she did not know where she belonged, or perhaps she felt that if she had been abandoned once it could happen again. What is clear is that Danielle was shocked and hurt, and, based on her relationship with her parents to that point, she had no reason to believe that they would be receptive to hearing about her reaction to the news. In fact, she felt that they were 'paranoid' that she might find her biological mother and return to her. Danielle found that she could not simply ignore her feelings; they were far too powerful. In her fright and confusion, the only means she had of adequately expressing her intensity of feeling was anger, and the most meaningful method of expressing that anger was to put even more distance between herself and her parents. Thus, she 'packed [her] little bag' and went through the motions of leaving. Of course, her parents prevented her from actually leaving her home, but they did not give her other reassurances of their love for her. A rift was created, and, ultimately, they were unable to prevent her from exercising the only power she had – refusing their parenting. Miller states that, 'if a child *can turn* to her parents and then experience some acceptance of her distress and some responsiveness,' she and the parents may be able to turn a potentially disconnecting interaction around.[12] Thus, if Danielle had been able to turn to her parents, express her distress, and elicit some responsiveness, she might have been able to continue to accept their parenting. Alternatively, if they had been able to invite her expressions of distress at that point, the outcome might also have been more favourable. That did not occur, and, as a result, Danielle acted out the depth of her hurt by making a point of disobeying them.

In her isolation, anger, neediness, and determination to disobey her parents, Danielle became an easy mark for Sandy and his sexual inclinations. The transformation of first Sandy's and then Peter's 'love' to abuse fed her anger, and she eventually lost sight of the initial hurt. Long past hurt, she became consumed with anger.

Danielle said, 'I'm a very, very angry person. I'm angry at the world in a way ... like, why me? I just tried to defend myself and I'm here.' In the absence of relationships in which she could express, clarify, and master her feelings, her anger grew. Years after she had left school, she was still hurt by the nuns' treatment of her. 'I'd love to see them and ask them "Why? Why did you treat me this way?" 'Cause I was the only one they would treat this way.' The children, now adults, who had harassed her at school were also the objects of her wrath.

The people that hurt me at school are still back home and whenever I see them I go really tense and the ideas go through my mind like, 'Oh, I'd like to revenge myself; you hurt me so bad.' Every time I would see them, I would feel the anger.

Danielle fantasized revenge against those who had hurt her.

... the idea that I would run them over – that was one of the best ideas – or break up their marriage. Since they were so happy, I was tempted to phone and invent some stories.

By the time she and I met for the interviews, Danielle's anger was directed mainly at men, and she realized that her attack on Marc was a product of this generalized anger, fuelled by too much alcohol.

... out of fricking booze – my anger towards men in general, because since the day I've been drinking, I hate men – not hate men, but every time a man would even say something wrong, I wouldn't even think twice about taking a beer or a chair and smacking him all over.

During her abusive relationships, her parents continued to support Danielle in their fashion. As her anger towards men grew, she directed less anger towards her parents. Her father had threatened to disown her if she stayed with Sandy after he broke her jaw, and that ultimatum seemed to reassure Danielle that her parents cared about her – it provided evidence of caring and of anger on her behalf. It was apparent that, over time, she had begun to interpret her parents' consistent behaviour towards her as caring, and she reestablished a functional relationship with them, especially after her mother became ill and Danielle was called upon to help out. The process of caring for her mother, and her mother's acceptance of her help, seemed to allow Danielle to 'earn' her place in the family. However, despite this development in their relationship, Danielle's sense of belonging still seemed tenuous. The evidence of this was in her need to idealize her parents and make her biological mother the scapegoat.

In my own way, I deserved – like I always tell mom and dad 'I don't deserve you. You've been too good.' I said maybe if I would've been with my real mother, now I could appreciate how good you were to me.
Maybe my [biological] mom is an alcoholic, or a real bitch – who knows?

Danielle could explain her own behaviour only by linking it to her biological mother or father, thus protecting the parental relationships that were available to her.

Because I have to take from somebody – my mom or my real dad. 'Cause I wasn't brought up with this kind of hell in my life ... So there has to be something behind the blanket, behind the curtain that is back to my roots.

The stark differences she perceived between her and her sister – 'that's night, I'm day' – provided her with more evidence that her biological roots were somehow to blame for the direction of her life.

Several times in the interviews, Danielle suggested that she had needed punishment when she was a child, and that perhaps, if her parents had punished her, she would not have run away with Sandy. Like Vicki, who, in asking for punishment from her grandparents, was in fact asking for limits to be set, Danielle was asking for some underlying wish to be satisfied. It was unlikely that she wanted to be hurt; rather, being punished by her parents may have meant, to her, that she really belonged to them. She interpreted their failure to punish her as stemming from a fear that she might run away – which would suggest, conversely, that if they had been secure in their relationship with her, they could have risked punishing her. It followed that, if her parents doubted the security of the relationship, then she, too, as the child, would have to doubt it.

Walker suggests that 'there is no real difference in psychological makeup between battered women who kill and those who do not.' She argues that most of the women in both groups are 'average' women and that the difference between them lies in the extent of the violence to which they have been subjected.[13] It must be noted, however, that, in reality, the difference can lie in other factors as well – factors that are entirely outside the women's control. Danielle's story is a good example. Marc came very close to dying because he received inappropriate treatment at the first hospital to which he was taken. If he had died, Danielle would have become a 'killer,' despite being the same person and having committed the same act. While this observation is not meant to minimize the seriousness of Danielle's action, the issue of extraneous factors is an important point to consider in view of the artificial division that the judicial system makes between killers and nonkillers, including women who kill their batterers and those who assault them without killing them. The fact that the batterer dies does not automatically mean that the woman is a more violent person.[14] Moreover, since, as Walker claims, there are no psychological differences between women who kill their batterers and those who do not, studies of the former can also be used to gain an understanding of the latter.

Walker,[15] Browne,[16] and Armstrong[17] discuss the effects of severe battering on women and suggest that an appropriate comparison can be made between women who have been battered and survivors of a disaster such as war. It has been found that battered women who have experienced repeated and unpredictable abuse exhibit a variety of symptoms characteristic of Posttraumatic Stress Disorder (PTSD), among which are hypervigilance and an exaggerated startle response.[18] Walker observes that, when a woman is severely battered, she may no longer be able to predict the outcome of her responses, and therefore 'chooses only responses that have a high probability of protecting her.'[19] Moreover, most people who have been subjected to such experiences 'tend to develop certain psychological symptoms that continue to affect their ability to function long after the original trauma.[20]

Although Danielle did not have a history of being battered in her relationship with Marc, she was clearly suffering from the effects of previous abusive relationships and was particularly vigilant for signs of potential abuse. She was determined to avoid another battering relationship and, when she felt threatened by Marc, she responded with a knee-jerk reaction against further abuse. Her behaviour was essentially the outcome of the hypervigilance and the predisposition to an intense startle response that had developed over the course of her previous relationships.

EXPRESSION OF EMOTION THROUGH ANGER

For all three women, anger was a secondary emotion. When Vicki was unable to express her true feelings of hurt and depression, she became angry instead, an emotion that was more 'acceptable' on the reserve. Doris's anger grew out of her feelings of rejection and loneliness. She was unable to express her true feelings precisely because she had been rejected and abandoned: those experiences were her proof that revealing her needs would *not* lead to having them met. Danielle's initial feelings of confusion, hurt, and fear surrounding the issue of her adoption were quickly transformed to anger because they were too threatening. She had never had the opportunity to learn that the intensity of such feelings can be lessened by sharing them.

At the source of the women's anger was their need to achieve or maintain connectedness with loved ones, and the hurt, depression, confusion, and sadness they experienced when satisfaction of that need was threatened or when the need went unfulfilled. They may have been especially vulnerable to the threat of disconnection because they had all lost their biological parents as infants, and the fear of loss was ever-present. Vicki valued her relationship with her grandmother, who had been her primary caregiver, but she also wanted to establish a stronger bond with her mother. She saw no need to relinquish one for the other, and she had no desire to do so. However, discomfort with a language of caring prevailed in her environment, and she was unable to express either the love she felt towards her grandmother or the hurt she felt at the banishment.

Brant has stated that Native 'tribes' observe an ethic of non-interference, which 'promotes positive interpersonal relations by discouraging coercion of any kind' and is made operational through the practice of emotional restraint.[21] Vicki's reluctance to express her most sensitive feelings to her grandmother may well have been determined by this cultural prohibition. Discussing her private thoughts and feelings was not familiar or comfortable for her, as she stated during our interviews. She was obviously conflicted about revealing her feelings, needing to discuss issues of importance but feeling inhibited because she was unaccustomed to self-disclosure.

Doris's situation was different from Vicki's in that her foster mother died when Doris was seven, and she never had anything resembling a mutually empathic relationship with a caregiver again. Her sense of being unloved and unlovable was generalized into chronic anger, which became the driving force in her interactions with other people.

Danielle lived in emotional isolation from her parents, and when she found out from other children that she had been adopted, she had no way of expressing her hurt to her parents.

As a society, we are not accustomed to dealing with women who engage in visible expressions of their anger. There are many accounts of women's victimization, but discourse on women as angry aggressors is very limited. As Bernardez points out, women's expression of anger is prohibited because it deviates from the stereotypical feminine ideal of passivity.[22] Thus, we know how to revile a male batterer and how to blame or sympathize with a victim of battering (depending on our degree of awareness and our politics), but we do not know how to respond to a woman who fights back. Doris admitted, with some pride, that she was a fighter. Indeed, each of the women in this study 'fought back' in some way, and each admitted to being angry. If visible anger and a willingness to fight on their own behalf are perceived in our society as aberrant in women, it is within the realm of possibility that women might be persecuted for displaying anger and for refusing to wear the 'feminine' cloak of passivity. Perhaps, in some cases, women are arrested in error for this very reason, particularly if they are members of a disparaged social group, such as recipients of social assistance or a racial or ethnic minority.

There has been considerable discourse in the criminology literature regarding conformity to the feminine ideal – the expectation that women are passive, compliant, and dependent – as a factor contributing to the lesser involvement of women than of men in criminality. While emphasizing that the findings have not been definitive, Naffine observes that 'feminine expectations at least partly account for female conformity in that they are associated with a tendency to greater commitment and attachment to conventional others.'[23] Although, judging by their actions, none of the women described here seemed to conform to a feminine stereotype of passivity, their nonconformity to the female role does not adequately explain their actions.

Vicki did conform to the customs that governed the expression of personal feelings among her people, a fact that raises the question of the need for cultural analysis. (It is not clear whether the customs applied to men and women in the same way.) Although it is unlikely that aggressiveness was officially condoned on Vicki's reserve, the ethic of non-interference that Brant describes, if it was, in fact, followed by the community, may have been interpreted by some as permission to be violent.[24] The principle of non-interference may be effective in a culture that is functioning optimally, but Vicki's band was not doing so. Therefore, as she herself implied, her lawbreaking activities with her teenage friends were inadvertently being reinforced by her grandparents' noninterference. Moreover, the tension produced by the practice of emotional restraint sometimes resulted in angry explosions of emotion.

Doris's angry outbursts and fighting approach were reinforced by the results they produced. For someone so deprived of empathic human interaction, the simple outcome of gaining attention can be a powerful reinforcer. Consequently, Doris began to see aggressiveness as her way of getting what she wanted, and she used it as a defence against her vulnerability.

Despite obvious cultural differences, both Vicki and Doris acted out in anger because they were unable to express their true feelings, particularly their need and longing for connection, and because their aggressiveness had been reinforced on many occasions.

Like most women, Danielle conformed intermittently to the stereotypical female role. As a child, she worked with her father in the barn, not with her mother in the kitchen. As a newly married seventeen-year-old, she wanted to do what was expected of a new wife but found that she was inadequately prepared for kitchen duties. She did the best she could and learned to enjoy her domestic accomplishments. She said that a good day was one in which she cleaned the house and had something freshly baked waiting for her children when they arrived home after school. In her relationships with abusive men, she learned to assume the expected feminine role of passivity after discovering that fighting back only increased the severity of the abuse she received. Danielle seemed to conform to the role to the extent that she was able, but the psychological effects of the abuse she had experienced overrode her belief that fighting back was ill-advised: the abuse ultimately forced her to deviate from the 'feminine' role.

When she was young, Danielle acted out in anger when her sense of connection with her parents was severed and she was unable to express her need and longing for connection with them. The eventual repercussions of her sense of disconnection led to situations in which she had to defend herself and in which her anger, rooted in fear, manifested itself as aggressiveness.

Their visible expression of anger brought these women into conflict with the law. Their actions, though extreme, should be seen as an expression of their hurt, depression, loneliness, confusion, and fear. When viewed as a secondary emotion that reflects the intensity of the underlying primary emotions, their anger gives evidence of the extreme pain that lay at the root of their actions.

6

The Women's Words: Fear

Fear was implicit in the stories of all the women I interviewed. For one woman, Lynne, fear for her own safety was transformed into a fear of her own aggressiveness, which became a reality when she fatally injured her foster daughter.

LYNNE

Lynne, a Caucasian woman of twenty-nine, described herself as 'dependent,' and as someone who copes 'by just going on.' She said she always felt like a 'misfit' in her family and that she didn't belong. Her only sense of belonging came from her strong association with the church.

Lynne had been severely abused and suffered profound psychological effects from that abuse, including a fear of her own aggression. She grew up in a household filled with violence, which began shortly after her family moved to Canada, when she was seven years old. Soon after they arrived, her father was severely injured in a fall at work, and the family concluded that the impact 'disrupted something in his brain,' causing the angry outbursts that subsequently became commonplace in the home. He became extremely abusive. 'I saw him take a baseball bat to my brother and – he never hit me, but – I saw him knock my mother to the floor and beat my brothers.' Although Lynne's father never hit her, she kept waiting for him to do so. 'I think I felt – don't I deserve it? Everybody else that's in the family got it. When's my turn?' When she watched her father beat her mother for the first time, she said, 'the fear was, if he swung at her for the first time ever, my turn can't be far behind.' Thus, Lynne lived in a climate of fear, as did her mother and brothers.

When he used to come home from work, the kids would scatter to their rooms, my mother would scatter to the kitchen, and we would listen at the door to see what kind of mood he was in. If he was in a good mood, we came out of our rooms. If he was in a bad mood, we stayed in our rooms until dinner time – because nobody wanted to be on the receiving end – now it's unfortunate my mother always had to be there, um – but to have fear – to have to listen on the other side of the door as to whether or not you could go out and say 'Hi' to your father, you know, it's really hard to describe to people the type of – you know, at any moment the backhand can be across your face and you haven't done anything.

As a defence, hypervigilance became a way of life for Lynne; she was always attuned to any threat of violence. Although violence against her always seemed imminent to Lynne, her father never struck her. Indeed, he paid little attention of any kind to her, and she believed he never wanted her. 'When I was born, my father wanted a boy. "Oh, it's a girl" – kind of trash her. Never bothered with me, never took me out in the stroller, nothing like that.' Lynne grew up feeling that she didn't exist in her father's eyes. She began to feel that a beating such as those that the rest of the family received would have proved otherwise. Whatever method she used to try to get his attention – good grades in school, for example – failed. Her father's favourite son, Brian, was the recipient of the most – and the worst – beatings. It was as though her father had only one child, and 'he wanted this boy to be so much like him that he created the anger in Brian.'

Her father succeeded in passing his violent behaviour on to Brian, and when her father and her mother separated, Brian declared himself 'the head of the household' and took it upon himself to deal out punishment. Lynne was her brother's primary target, and he beat her twice a week for two years. He threatened to kill her if she told anyone, and so the violence proceeded unchecked.

My brother was like my father. He hit where you can't see. The black eye was the one time that he erred, and that was when my mother was in Europe. We were being watched by a neighbour and she [mother] doesn't know where it ever came from. Kitchen knives are missing and she [mother] never found out where they went. They were in Brian's room. At any time they came out, and that's the scary thing – to know that even when you close your door to go to bed at night you're not safe, because Brian's got a knife under his mattress.

During the reign of terror, Lynne received no emotional support. On the contrary, another brother sometimes assisted Brian in beating her. Because of the family's frequent moves, Lynne was unable to form close friendships, and, in any case, she never felt comfortable bringing other children home because of 'what may be happening there.' Usually, she managed to develop one friendship in each different school she attended, but Lynne always remained detached from other people, and these friendships were never intimate enough that she could reveal the family secrets. Neither did Lynne receive or solicit support from her mother. She described her relationship with her mother as 'strange,' saying her mother treated her 'like a child' or, alternatively, that she and her mother were 'like sisters,' and that she was the older sister. Perhaps because her mother was suicidal following the separation from her father, Lynne never discussed the abuse with her. When these situations became too blatant to ignore, her mother chose to avoid taking sides. Her mother's 'neutrality' was quite likely motivated by a sense of powerlessness, resulting from the abuse she suffered first at the hands of her husband and later, after his departure, of Brian. None the less, Lynne felt that her mother should have done something about the violence. 'If somebody were coming at my child with a baseball bat, I'm sorry, I'd step in between.'

Because she felt constrained by Brian's threats and by her own feelings of humiliation, Lynne was unable to share her feelings about her family situation with anyone, and was therefore never able to test their validity. She grew up knowing that she did not want to be violent, like her father and brothers, but she also knew that she did not want to be as passive and denying as her mother. Unfortunately, she had no way of knowing how to integrate these intentions.

As she grew up in her violent and friendless home, Lynne was driven by two things: a strong need to be loved, and a fear of violence, which was always present. She had seen that love and abuse went hand in hand in her family, but she did not want that for herself. She found, however, that it was not easy to act in accordance with her wishes for a different kind of life. Like many who suffer severe abuse, Lynne had sustained psychological damage, and it had gone untreated. Like Danielle, Lynne exhibited numerous symptoms of Posttraumatic Stress Disorder: she had re-experienced the trauma in at least one near-psychotic episode; she avoided stimuli associated with the trauma she had experienced; and she was hypervigilant and very sensitive to noise and angry outbursts.

Lynne's hypervigilance interfered in her relationship with her husband.

My first year of marriage ... if we would go anywhere, if he wanted to put his

arm around me, he had to tell me ... because we were in a public party and he
went to put his arm around me and I flinched, and everybody in the room thought,
'Oh, he beats her' ... he looked at me like 'What are you doing?' I said, 'I thought
you were going to hit me,' and he said, 'I've never hit you.' I said, 'I know, but
it's been there in my past.'

Later, Lynne's fear took a bizarre turn, when, in a loud argument with
her husband, she suddenly 'saw' her father attacking her. The very thing
that Lynne had feared for so long seemed to be happening.

I had an experience where in an argument with my husband I thought he was my
father, and I retreated from him. He looked like my father, he sounded like my
father, to the point where my husband had to call my mother because he couldn't
comfort me, because the minute he stepped into the room, I screamed. That was
it, he was coming to get me.

Fear for her own safety was generalized to fear of what she might do –
fear of her own potential for aggressiveness – and she was unable to resolve this fear. Lynne worried, 'You have the father and the sons – when's
the daughter going to step in? I wasn't sure if it was heredity or not, and
I thought, if they do it, I could do it.' Lynne's fear of her own aggressiveness became reality when she fatally injured a child for whom she was
providing foster care. She felt that, where there had been one person, there
were now two distinct people, one the 'good girl' and one the 'bad girl.'

On one side of the wall is the good girl who loves her family, and on the other
side of the wall is the person who caused another person to die, and is here for
that. I think that's the only way, right now, that I can deal with the fact that I'm
here, is that *I'm* not here – I'm here but I'm not here.

It was as though she had lost control of the aggressive part of herself,
and that part had taken on a life of its own. When I asked her to describe
the appearance of the bad girl, it became obvious why she was determined
to maintain control over her emotions and why she feared her own aggressiveness. In response to my question, 'What does the bad girl look
like?' she answered,

My father with long hair. She's very big, somebody you would cross the street –
if you were walking down the street and she was coming at you, you would cross
the street to walk away from her. Not a very personable person. Somebody that
– pick your worst image, your worst nightmare of somebody, although not quite

to the monster status, but pretty close ... everything that could possibly be bad is there.

When I asked her what it was like to be the bad girl, she replied, 'Scary in some ways and other ways – power – I don't care, nobody can get inside me ... if she doesn't care, nobody can hurt her. If nobody can hurt her then she can survive.'

Lynne felt that the power of the bad girl could help her to survive, and on occasion she was empowered by it to stand up to her abusive brother or her father. However, she was fundamentally uncomfortable with feelings of power and seemed to believe that only a 'bad girl' would enjoy such feelings or tolerate her own anger. Her fear of her power, therefore, was instrumental in her use of passivity or avoidance to achieve rigid control over her fear and anger. She devised a method of controlling the potential for aggressiveness in herself that she experienced as so powerful: 'I will back away, walk away, anything ... to get out of the situation.' Lynne saw that her father and brothers were out of control, and she took precautions to avoid losing control of herself, especially with her children. She said, 'I will be in control by not being out of control.'

In her role as a mother, Lynne's need for love and her fear of her own aggressiveness were readily evident. On the one hand, she could give her children love and acceptance – which she felt would 'wipe out what I felt as a child' – and could receive love and acceptance from them in return. On the other hand, because of her constant fear of her own potential for aggressiveness, she felt the need to keep a tight rein on her emotions in her dealings with her children.

Miller points out that when 'a person cannot find ways to change the relationships available to her, she will take the only possible step: attempt to change the person [whom it is] possible to change — herself.'[1] Lynne learned from her childhood family relationships that she could not expect to change or control other people, so she took steps to control herself, even though she had no history of being abusive. In a manner that further constrained her ability to deal openly with her feelings of anger and fear, she consciously avoided encounters with her children in which she might inflict on them the terror of her own childhood, to the extent that she avoided even relatively innocuous behaviour such as raising her voice to them. She created clear guidelines – restrictions on herself – to protect her children.

When it comes to seeing the injury that anger can cause, you just say, 'I'll never – ,' and in all my years I've never done that. I've removed myself, I've hidden behind a door, or put that other person in the room or in their crib, or I've stepped across into a room to draw that line and say, 'I need a little bit of space.' If I'm not able to deal with him, like if I was angry, I would place him in his room if he couldn't get there under his own steam. It was just, 'Please, get away from me. I'm angry with you but that's my fault, not yours. Please, get away from me.'

Lynne recoiled at the thought of being responsible for the death of her foster child, Dinah. She said that, when she was arrested, she repeated to herself, 'That's not me, that's not true, that can't possibly be true. I wouldn't do that.'

Lynne did not know why her usual strategy of 'removing' herself had failed her on the day she fatally injured Dinah. She wondered, 'Is it something in me that just clicked, that just shut off because I couldn't take it any more?' The tight rein she had kept on her feelings had apparently snapped.

Lynne did not remember feeling particularly pressured that day, but she did describe some confusion about her level of stress. She had been informed that Dinah's permanent home was ready, and that the child would therefore be leaving her in a few days. Lynne reasoned that the situation was working out well for everyone concerned, but, emotionally, the loss she felt was greater than she had been prepared to admit. She said, 'I became very attached to Dinah, more than I realized.' In order to understand the nature of Lynne's attachment to the child, it was necessary to delve into the details of a miscarriage she had suffered several months before Dinah's arrival.

Lynne described herself as the type of person who, from the minute she knows she is pregnant, 'talk[s] to the babies to let them know they're wanted.' She also told her children, as soon as she knew she was pregnant that last time, that they could expect a sibling, so she and the family were caught up in the anticipation of a new baby very early in the pregnancy. Lynne's feelings about this pregnancy were complicated by the memory of her experience with a previous pregnancy, which she had considered terminating. She and her husband had been experiencing marital difficulties at the time, and she had not been sure that she could deal with another child. She decided against the abortion (in part because of her religious beliefs), but she retained some feelings of guilt for having even considered ending the pregnancy. In addition, the daughter she had considered aborting always seemed to prefer her father, which exacerbated Lynne's guilt feelings. Thus, when she miscarried the last pregnancy, she was profoundly affected. Because of her feelings of unworthiness, she experienced the miscarriage as a 'rejection.' 'It was kind of like I'm not worthy of this child and also that the child didn't want me as a mother, or to come into this family.' Lewis suggests that 'mourning stillbirth is difficult because although there is a sense of loss, there is little sense of having lost some-*body*.'[2] Whereas mourning normally involves recalling memories of a person, mourning a stillbirth or miscarriage involves giving up wishes, hopes, and fantasies.[3] Indeed, the loss is experienced as a loss of a part of oneself more than as the loss of a physically distinct other, so that the woman may experience 'more intense self-denigration and inner emptiness with perinatal loss than with other types of losses,' as well as shame, guilt, and anger at having been cheated.[4]

Despite her own feelings about the miscarriage, Lynne's greatest concern was her children's sense of loss, which she assumed was as great as her own, and she did everything she could to make it easier for them. In the process of caring for her children, she ignored her own need to explicitly and fully mourn her loss, which clearly, she needed to do.

Every time I'd had pain I'd had something to show for it. Now I just had this big hole in my heart that there wasn't anything there anymore, and I'd just sit and cry – you know, diaper commercials and baby food commercials would just set me off.

Her spontaneous bouts of crying did not constitute a completion of the grieving process, however, and instead of recognizing that she needed to mourn the lost child, Lynne tried to 'forget' that she had been pregnant. On the heels of the miscarriage, Dinah's arrival was welcomed with joy.

She just fit right in ... it was just like everything that everybody needed to fill this gap where this child should have been ... in my heart it was my child.

In studies of women who have experienced the loss of a child through stillbirth, miscarriage, or neonatal death, it has been found that the women who became pregnant again within six months of the loss had difficulty distinguishing their dead infant from the expected infant because, 'like identical twins until you know them, one foetus is much like another.'[5] Pregnancy can also inhibit the grieving process when it immediately follows a miscarriage. For Lynne, it seemed that the expected child had arrived, grieving was unnecessary, and she had the opportunity to redeem her image of herself as a good and worthy mother.

I think I tried to fill a hole with Dinah, and tried to block out that it [the miscarriage] ever happened, because I couldn't acknowledge that it had happened. My love and everything was ready to give to this child that I miscarried, but then she [Dinah] came to my home and she got all this extra that I was wanting to give to the child I lost. So she just fit right in.

For Lynne, Dinah became a member of the family. 'It became part of normal to have her there.' But the attachment went beyond including Dinah as a member of the family. Lynne loved the child and expressed concern, during the interviews, that she might have been 'a little too possessive' of her.

Given Lynne's attachment to Dinah, it seemed that her impending loss may have rekindled the feelings of rejection, guilt, loss, and unworthiness that she had experienced after the miscarriage but had never completely worked through. 'Maybe, in the back of my mind, that was another punishment.'

Of course, the fact that Lynne was losing another child, traumatic as it may have been, does not explain her actions. The question that Lynne asked – 'If I loved her, why did I hurt her?' – remains unanswered.

INTERGENERATIONAL TRANSFER OF VIOLENCE

Social learning theory has been helpful in developing an understanding of the ways in which violence is transmitted from generation to generation. According to the theory, children observe, then imitate, the behaviour of others.[6] Certainly, Lynne did reproduce violent behaviour that was similar in intensity to the behaviour she had witnessed in childhood. Given the complexity of her situation, however, imitation alone is insufficient as an explanation of her attack on Dinah. In her research with women, Korbin found that an important factor in determining how violence is repeated from generation to generation is the meaning that the women assign to the abuse they experience.[7] For Lynne, abuse was terrifying from two perspectives – that of a victim and that of a potential aggressor.

Miller points out that when the only relationships available are ones in which it is impossible to relate in a mutually empathic and, thus, growth-enhancing manner, a person is forced to keep more and more of herself out of her relationships. These parts of a person that are withheld from relationships remain unchanged by experience.[8] Lynne kept the angry and fearful parts of herself out of her relationships, and excluded from her experience, they could not develop or change. Instead, they remained similar to the fear and anger of a child, untempered by adult methods of dissipation. Just as Miller postulates, Lynne reached a point at which she was able to tolerate only certain feelings in herself and others. She was unable to tolerate anger in others; indeed, she experienced a brief disso-ciative, or, frankly, psychotic, reaction when arguing with her husband, and she was very careful to control angry interactions between her chil-dren. Unable to tolerate anger in herself, she could not accept a less-than-ideal image of herself as a mother. However, that perfect image was marred when she considered aborting one child, then miscarried another. When Dinah arrived to replace the child she miscarried, Lynne's percep-tion of herself as a loving, competent, worthy mother was restored. Then, with the impending loss of Dinah, her feelings of unworthiness and rejec-tion resurfaced. She felt ashamed at her failure and powerless to change the situation. As Caplan postulates, feelings that cannot be tolerated are often replaced with anger. On the day she injured Dinah, Lynne's anger erupted and took the form of violence that she had learned in childhood, a form against which she had spent her life rigidly defending.[9]

Although Lynne thought it would be best for Dinah to be given a per-manent home, her cognitive controls were insufficient to counter the un-acknowledged rage that she must have been experiencing. It is possible, on the one hand, that she felt rage at her own lost child, for leaving her. On the other hand, just as some mothers of stillborns have been known to experience anger towards a surviving child, she may have been angry at Dinah for living while her own child failed to survive.[10] Despite her valiant efforts of so many years to avoid repeating the violence she had experienced as a child, she was unable, at that moment in her life, to maintain the rigid controls she had learned to rely upon.

In Korbin's research with nine women, each of whom had been im-prisoned for the fatal abuse of one of her children, she found that the women's childhoods were characterized by 'a preponderance of risk fac-tors and a relative absence of supports or compensating factors.'[11] The risk factors included a history of having been abused.

In thinking about Lynne's case, it was important to remember that the abuse that had had the greatest impact on her was the abuse she had witnessed, as perpetrated by her father. For Lynne, witnessing the abuse of her brothers meant that she was unequivocally the outsider in her fam-ily, unworthy even of her father's wrath. In her position as a psycholog-ically but not physically abused child, she was profoundly alone. Lynne became determined to redress the wrongs visited upon her by raising her own children differently, so she set strict guidelines for coping with her children to avoid repeating the abuse.

One important theme in the literature on child abuse is that abusive parents tend to treat their children as though they were much more mature than they really are.[12] Studies have also shown that abusive mothers have difficulty empathizing with their children.[13] Earlier, I outlined the importance of empathy in women's development and indicated that the capacity for empathy develops in a relational context. Lynne did not have the developmental advantage of empathic relationships in her childhood, and, as a result, the struggle to be empathic with her own children was especially difficult. Paradoxically, although her intention to raise her children differently from the way she had been raised was necessary if there was to be any hope of halting the intergenerational transfer of violence, the very fact that it was rooted in 'wiping out' the wrongs of her own childhood created a problem. Lynne very much wanted to create loving relationships with her children for the express purpose of their nurturance, and, to her credit, she had been successful in keeping violence out of their lives. However, she was unable to let go of her own fear, anger, and hurt, and simply to focus on her relationship with her children. It seemed that Lynne was partly – but powerfully – motivated by the notion that if her children, including Dinah, thrived, perhaps she would as well.

In this context, it is possible to understand that, given the other stress-inducing factors in her life, the prospect of losing Dinah, whose presence had eased her feelings of failure, was too much for Lynne. She may have experienced a moment of uncooperative behaviour as a deliberate assault upon her, with the result that she lost the tight control on which she depended to harness the aggressiveness that so frightened her.

7

Relationship, Empowerment, and Lawbreaking

Hearing the women's reasons for their conflicts with the law and reflecting on the contributing factors that were evident in their stories led me to a second stage of understanding. Keeping in mind women's developmental needs and their position in the social structure, I studied the network of feelings, thoughts, events, and people that the women discussed, and uncovered two implicit themes that appeared in each woman's story. These themes, the centrality of relationships to the women's lives and the struggle for instrumentality or empowerment, are the common threads uniting their stories. These themes were evident throughout the women's experiences and were the keys to understanding the interaction between their psychological development and their social world.

CENTRALITY OF RELATIONSHIPS TO THE WOMEN'S LIVES

In her critique *Female Crime: The Construction of Women in Criminology*, Naffine points out that there has been an enduring belief that delinquency among girls is precipitated by their failure to win relationships with boys.[1] Although the women I interviewed wanted positive affective relationships, they did not discuss their major relational concerns in terms of acquiring relationships with men. Rather, the women voiced concerns about repairing and maintaining connections with the people who were close to them, especially parents and children.[2]

In her empirical work with girls, Morris retained the principle of goal orientation described by Merton in his strain theory, but postulated a general goal of positive relationships with family members and boyfriends.[3] If Morris had been less concerned about proving goal frustration, she might have placed more importance on her finding that nondelinquent girls were more likely to talk things over with their mothers than were delinquent girls. This emphasis on connection with the mother goes to the heart of the relational theory of women's development, but Morris did not explore the nature of the connection between delinquent girls' criminality and their lack of communication with their mothers.

If there was an element of frustration for the fourteen women in the present study, it lay in their struggle to retain existing relationships or to connect with important others in the hope of moving towards empowering development. Some of the women had suffered severe losses of relationships, some were trying to forestall such losses, some had suffered prolonged pain and disconnection in relationships, some were protesting others' desecration of and inadequacy in their relationships, and one was afraid to become fully present in her relationships with her children.

The women's attempts to maintain connection took a variety of forms. The women whose reason for coming into conflict with the law was 'need' accepted the expectations and values of others so that they would, in turn, be accepted; the women whose reason was 'disconnection' insulated themselves so they could set aside the pain of physical and emotional disconnection from important others and create a fantasy of nurturing relationships or preserve, in the form of internal images, any positive element that might have been present in their earlier relationships; the women whose theme was 'anger' responded to rejection, anger, or violence with anger in their quest to be understood; and the woman whose theme was 'fear' set rigid boundaries around the aggressiveness that she felt she shared with her father and brothers in order to ensure her children's safety in their connection with her.

The women's struggles to repair and maintain relationships were individual and complex. In my exploration of the women's 'need,' it became apparent that Marianne, Jacqueline, Connie, Arlene, and Rose were attempting to sustain relationships by meeting the expectations of important others. It was their hope that by being the way they believed their families and society wanted them to be, they would earn a better connection with those important others. They believed that society, and their families, expected them to be self-sufficient, responsible for their children, materially successful, and undemanding, and they internalized those expectations. However, they encountered many hazards in their attempts to meet their needs and fulfil their expectations of themselves. Men who had economic power over them withheld the support to which they were entitled, paid them inadequately and unfairly for their work, and used their influence over them for their own purposes; men who saw the women's need took advantage of them.

Meeting the expectations of important others seemed to be the only way the women felt they could sustain relationships with them. It was the difference between their own and others' expectations and what they understood as their 'ability' to live in accordance with those expectations that they experienced as need.

The women whose reason for lawbreaking was 'disconnection' (Margaret, Doreen, Penny, Sarah, and Bonnie) had suffered extreme pain in important relationships. As my understanding of them developed, I came to see that, in their attempts to keep the relationships alive, they insulated themselves from their pain by using drugs and alcohol. People who were important to them abandoned them, abused them, humiliated them, manipulated them, or disappointed them in very significant ways. Sometimes those important others made the women do things that were harmful to them. Nevertheless, the women tried to hold on to the relationships because they were all they had. However, the women were damaged and alienated, and the pain was too much for them to bear; they had to stop caring and hoping with such intensity. By chance or by emulating those around them, they found ways to relieve some of the pain with drugs, and, at the same time, they found other people who were as needy as they were. Even though they could connect with these people only around the drugs, they shared a common purpose with them. Finding such people and using drugs helped them to forget some of the original pain some of the time. However, none of this helped them to improve their actual connections with the people who were most important to them, or to find more positive relationships. What the drugs did enable them to do was to maintain, in their imaginations, more satisfactory connections with the people who were important to them.

Exploring the stories of Vicki, Doris, and Danielle, who exhibited 'visible anger,' I found that they, too, had suffered pain in important relationships, but that they were still trying to sustain a real connection. They had been rejected and abused by their caregivers and other people in their lives. They felt lost, unloved, and powerless to win love, understanding, and security. They had lived in a world of isolation, violence, and alienation from others. Even though they suffered a great deal, they still longed for connection with someone important to them. They kept trying to make connections even though their attempts were repeatedly met with rejection, abuse, misunderstanding, or the threat of abandonment. Perhaps to avoid the pain of these failed attempts, they became very angry. Sometimes they were unable to contain that anger, and they struck out. When they did that, important others sometimes noticed and reacted to them.

Lynne, whose 'fear' was the driving force of her life, was also abused.

She thought long and hard about the abuse that she had witnessed and endured, and reasoned – and greatly feared – that if other members of her family could be so violent, there must be a part of her that could become violent as well. Above all, she wanted to avoid replicating the violence herself. To that end, she employed a method that hinged on her childhood experiences, in which she separated herself from the source of the violence. In adulthood, whenever she felt anger, she would establish boundaries between herself and those she cared for most. Her ability to manage herself well with her children had been her main source of pride. On one occasion, however, her ability to step behind the protective 'line,' as she usually did, failed her.

In each of these explanations, the reasons expressed by the women become even more meaningful when the importance, to them, of relationships is understood. Clearly, the relationships they described were central to their lives and strongly influenced the course their lives had taken.

In her paper 'Connections, Disconnections and Violations,' Miller discusses the importance of relationships and the terror of isolation.

The most terrifying and destructive feeling that a person can experience is isolation ... feeling locked out of the possibility of human connection. This feeling of desperate loneliness is usually accompanied by the feeling that you, yourself, are the reason for the exclusion. It is because of *who* you are. And you feel helpless, powerless, unable to act to change the situation. People will do almost anything to escape this combination of condemned isolation and powerlessness.[4]

Through examinations of the ways in which women develop in the context of relationships, the Stone Center group has found that mutual empathy is the mechanism by which contacts become affirming and growth-enhancing connections. The notion of mutuality is integral to the process.

The important relationships in the lives of the women in this study were starkly lacking in mutual empathy. The important people in these women's lives abused, abandoned, or neglected them; they had impossible expectations of the women or made demands on them that were self-serving. Under such conditions, empathy could neither be given nor received. Although the women made many attempts to elicit empathic – and connecting – responses from the significant others in their lives, they usually did not succeed. Their attempts were rarely met with adequate, similar responses.

Where there is an imbalance of empathy, a 'devaluing of the self and resentment of the other, who comes to be seen as powerful and more worthy,' may occur.[5] An exact 'measure' of empathy is impossible, however, so the specific nature of the 'imbalance' in the relationships of the women in this study with their important others cannot be determined. None the less, a lack of mutuality was certainly implicit in the situations they described: all the women were either trying to live up to the expectations of others or were subordinated to the others' self-involved behaviours and deprived of any consideration of their own needs. Because of the resulting devaluation of themselves, the women were vulnerable to those who would prey on them, to threats against their tenuous security, and to illusions of emotional support. In the absence of mutual caring, survival became the focus. According to Gilligan, survival is 'the ultimate self-protective stance.'[6]

Relationships organized around a core of mutual empathy were missing from the lives of the women, making them vulnerable to the demands of anyone who held the promise, however illusory, of a mutually empathic relationship or of the means to acquire one.

THE STRUGGLE FOR INSTRUMENTALITY AND EMPOWERMENT

The women in this study grew up in situations which, in one way or another, left them feeling alone and emotionally, if not physically, disconnected from growth-affirming interactions with others. Though the circumstances and women's methods varied at different stages of life, it became apparent that they were responding to the disconnections they had experienced by waging struggles for emotional and, sometimes, physical survival. They were engaged in battles to ward off feelings of isolation and accompanying feelings of powerlessness. Confronted with chaotic and alienating situations, they used whatever means were available to reduce the sense of powerlessness they felt and to somehow bring about more desirable responses from important others. When they were children, this may have meant running away or stealing small items from stores. In adulthood, the struggle for a sense of instrumentality was often implicit in the women's denial of abuse or victimization, their refusal to confide in others, or, paradoxically, their submission to the wishes and expectations of others. By denying victimization and refusing to confide in others, the women may have maintained a sense of themselves as nearer-to-equal partners in their relationships. Submitting to the wishes and expectations of others may have been a way of making an impact on others, a way of experiencing themselves as instrumental and important in relationships. Stiver suggests that when children grow up in dysfunctional families, being authentic and empathic can be dangerous, so they learn to stay out of relationships while behaving as though they are participating in them.[7] The women in this study may have learned that by denying victimization and submitting to the wishes and expectations of others, they were able to maintain an appearance of being in relationships without exposing their vulnerabilities in situations in which exposure would be dangerous for them.

Marianne, Jacqueline, Connie, Arlene, and Rose, who believed their lawbreaking to be a function of need, had internalized their family's – and society's – concept of what it means to be instrumental in directing one's life. This concept is rooted in an ideology of materialism and individualism. The women had been told many times, in many ways, that they should be able to take charge of their lives and their circumstances, and live up to a socially prescribed standard as interpreted by family members. They believed that they should be able to do so no matter what their limitations in terms of education or opportunity or support. Having internalized social and familial concepts of instrumentality, they felt responsible and in control when they were able to meet the needs and expectations of important others. It was then that they felt, temporarily, like adults with rightful places in the world. Thus reinforced, the women continued to struggle to meet the same demands and expectations through whatever means they saw were available to them, even if the available means were not socially sanctioned.

Margaret, Doreen, Penny, Sarah, and Bonnie, for whom 'disconnection' was at the root of lawbreaking, had experienced emotional pain so severe that it became central to their existence and made them feel as though their lives were out of their control. They dealt with their pain and their feelings of incontinence by numbing themselves with drugs. When they used drugs, they could eclipse the pain and forget that they did not have control of their lives. By learning how to procure a steady supply of painkiller for their bodies, they felt as though they had some control; they were able to regulate their activities towards the goal of maintaining their supply of the needed drugs, and they then had a purpose and a steady diversion. By regulating their activities, they were able to ensure that their bodies would not be wracked with the physical pain of withdrawal. It was much easier for them to manage this physical pain than their emotional pain.

Vicki, Doris, and Danielle felt powerless to effect positive or affirming responses in their relationships with important others. Their angry reactions were desperate attempts to make an impact on others. They grew up wondering where they belonged. They raged at the rejection, misunderstanding, abuse, and humiliation that they continued to suffer. Their anger, which was in fact an expression of their feelings surrounding these problems, was overwhelming. Although they didn't want to hurt anyone, they couldn't tolerate the continuing assaults on their emotions or their persons, or both. They longed for relief from their anger; therefore, they felt that they must both express it and alert others to its strength. Sometimes, in the process of expressing their anger and alerting others to it, they hurt people or destroyed things.

Lynne was raised in a completely chaotic environment. She was forced to resort to the desperate measures of isolating herself and rigidly structuring her life in order to survive. She was terrified that she had become engulfed by her early environment, so she attempted to create safety for her children by continuing to exert rigid control over her own behaviour. However, the disconnection inherent in such rigidity and isolation meant that these controls were extremely fragile. After years of watching and experiencing abuse, she felt that it was a part of her, a part that terrified her. She was therefore unable to tolerate even the slightest hint of aggressiveness in herself, especially around her children. She learned to contain the part of herself that she feared by setting hard and fast boundaries around it, rather than learning to safely express her deepest feelings in the presence of others. When her rigid method of control gave way, the frightening part of her was unleashed in an unmodified state.

To summarize, the women struggled for instrumentality – in other words, they attempted to acquire a sense of power in their lives. They did this in several ways: by attempting to conform to society's material standards (which had been passed along to them through their caregivers, usually their parents); by finding ways to numb their pain; by striking out; and by creating rigid boundaries. However, none of these methods was satisfactory, and all ultimately failed to serve the best interests of the women. The women's attempts to achieve a sense of power were closely linked to the deficits in their relationships.

RELATIONSHIP AND EMPOWERMENT

Traditionally, power has been defined as forcefulness or control 'over' something or someone – a definition that is consistent with the hierarchically structured world in which we live. In *Women and Power*, Miller points out that women have a great deal of trouble embracing this traditional notion of power and therefore tend to reject it. She believes that, for women, power is an energy through which they foster growth in others. Based on this understanding, Miller offers a working definition of power that has greater relevance to women's experiences: she defines it as 'the capacity to produce change.'[8] According to this conceptualization, a woman gains a sense of her own power, or experiences empowerment, as she develops her ability to produce change or movement in another in the context of mutually empathic relationships.

Jordan emphasizes that reciprocality or mutuality is an important component of this conceptualization of empowerment; a woman must receive as well as give empathy in order to develop a sense of her own power. Where there is an imbalance of empathy, the other is viewed as more powerful (in the conventional sense) and more worthy. When a woman is the recipient of empathy, however, she is encouraged towards feelings of worthiness; as a giver of empathy, she experiences a sense of her own power to create change. This is a process that evolves over time, as the capacity for participation in mutually empathic relationships grows.[9]

According to Miller, in healthy relationships, women feel a sense of increased energy, which empowers them to 'act beyond the relationship.'[10] Healthy, mutually empathic relationships empower women to interact within society as if it were a growth-fostering environment. This ability to interact in the outside world as if the world were a growth-fostering environment is the mechanism by which women are able to move into new relationships with the expectation that those relationships will be empowering. It is also the mechanism that enables women to leave relationships that are not growth-enhancing. Women thus empowered expect to make an impact upon their environment and to receive the benefit of whatever others in their world have to offer.

It follows that a woman who has not had the benefit of relationships that are moving towards mutual empathy will neither feel worthy nor fully experience her own power. It is when a woman is disempowered in this way that she feels unable to make an impact on her personal or her social world; she is unable to develop the capacity to become fully functional in the world and retreats into unhealthy relationships and behaviours, through which she intermittently experiences the illusion of power.

THE INTERSECTION OF EMPATHY AND LAWBREAKING

Criminologists Ross and Fabiano propose that empathy may help to inhibit antisocial behaviour. Defining empathy as the ability to understand and share the feelings of others, they suggest that lawbreaking can be inhibited if lawbreakers are taught concern for other people and if they understand the effects of their own behaviour on others. Ross and Fabiano see empathy as an acquired skill incorporating cognitive and expressive elements that can be taught through cognitive exercises and modelling.[11]

Jordan's notion of empathy is more complex. She describes it as a process involving emotional responses as well as cognitive structuring. She believes that, to be empathic, one must have 'the basic capacity and motivation for human relatedness which allows perception of the other's affective cues ... followed by a surrender to affective arousal in oneself ... producing a temporary identification with the other's emotional state ... and a resolution period in which one regains a sense of separate self that understands what has just happened.'[12] For Jordan, empathy is a complex process requiring the resilient ego boundaries that are typical of a high level of psychological development. Optimally, one becomes flexible enough to experience the feelings of another while retaining the ability to discern and return to one's own distinct feeling state. Mutual empathy is a process whereby differences in the participants are validated.

Surrey points out that, although there are, indeed, teaching and learning elements in the development of empathy, much more is involved. A child begins to develop empathy when her feelings are attended to and responded to by another; the complex process through which mutual empathy develops is initiated in this way. Thus, the 'learning' of empathy is a reciprocal or, ideally, a mutual process; logically, this process begins for an individual when she interacts with another person who has benefited from mutually empathic relationships. In healthy development, empathy is a by-product as well as a facilitating mechanism of mutually empowering relationships.[13]

Ross and Fabiano fail to incorporate the notion of mutuality, rendering theirs an inchoate conceptualization of the development of empathy. Nevertheless, their point that empathy and law-abidingness are somehow connected is worth pursuing. This connection is best explored through an examination of the ways in which women's development within the gestalt of mutually empathic relationships intersects with their social world.[14]

Neither individuals nor relationships exist in a vacuum; whether mutually empathic or unbalanced in some way, they are fully embedded in their environment. Therefore, the kind of environment in which a relationship exists, both immediate and global, has an impact on the relationship. When the environment devalues what is essential to women's development, the impact is profound. In this society, the disempowerment of women is reinforced by the hierarchal society in which we live, both through the promulgation of images of power that are not relevant for most women and through a structure in which women easily become alienated from one another as their needs are subordinated to the social structure and its more powerful members. This is especially true for women who have not had the benefit of early, mutually empathic relationships. Disempowerment can occur when violence is perpetrated against women and when the function of relationships is devalued. The social world can thus be extremely disempowering for the woman who does not live her life with the benefit of mutually empathic relationships. If they are to become fully functional within society, women must be able to seek out those pockets of society that are friendly towards the notion of empowered women, to counteract the effects of a disempowering society.

When in a state of disempowerment, a woman may lose or fail to acquire an ability to recognize and accept empathic relationships, which results in her inability to experience herself as worthy. In severe cases, a woman may not trust another's empathic response to her, if she has become accustomed to being coerced through feigned caring, and abused. Although she is fearful of *empathic* relationships, she retains an inclination to seek out and hold on to people, because they embody the hope of real connection. However, to protect herself, she may act as though she is in a relationship without actually connecting authentically. She often finds herself in unhealthy relationships simply because they have a familiar quality. She may be unable to give up such relationships if she is able to generate reactions within them, because they represent hope, especially in their early stages. Her experience of disempowerment and her concomitant desire to experience empowerment may precipitate her initiation of or participation in antisocial, lawbreaking, acts through which she acquires a false sense of power.

The women in this study struggled to become empowered in relationships that were ordered around hurt, neglect, misunderstanding, fear, and other non-empathic characteristics. Because of the absence of mutually empathic relationships in their lives, they did not develop a sense of themselves as effective in the world. In desperation, they tried whatever means were available to develop a sense of their own (false) power.

When women are empowered through mutually empathic relationships, they are able to interact with the larger world as though it were a growth-fostering environment. The women interviewed for this study understood, at some level, that the vehicle to their empowerment lay in their relationships. In their struggles to empower themselves and to experience them-selves as effective in the world, they attempted to retain, sustain, or protect the relationships that were available to them. The available relationships were often exploitive, abusive, unstable, or rooted in the misconceptions about women that prevail in this society and reflect its culture. The women were deprived of the mutual empathy needed for empowerment, and their resulting perceived and real disempowerment was reflected in their feel-ings of need, disconnection, anger, and fear. In their attempts to achieve a sense of empowerment, they were led into conflict with the law.

8

Reconceptualizing Women's Lawbreaking

In *Thou Shalt Not Be Aware: Society's Betrayal of the Child*, Alice Miller discusses Quentin Bell's biography of Virginia Woolf. Bell describes Woolf's 'schizophrenic episodes,' beginning at the age of twelve, and her suicide, at the age of fifty-nine. He also reveals that, from the age of four to puberty, she was 'sexually molested' on an almost daily basis by a much older half-brother. Bell concludes that he doesn't know whether the trauma had any permanent effect on Woolf. In response to this, Miller comments: 'How can an author who describes with great empathy Woolf's trauma and the entire dishonest atmosphere surrounding it at the same time question its importance? One would think that by now such an obvious compartmentalization of knowledge would be a thing of the past.'[1]

By the same token, how is it that criminologists have been able to describe the need of female lawbreakers, the effect of other people on them, their anger, and sometimes even their fear, without seeing the obvious, that – if the fourteen women in this study are in any way representative – women who come into conflict with the law, like all of us, want to connect, belong, and feel and be effective. Rather than acknowledging the core homology that exists between 'them' and 'us,' criminologists have tended to compartmentalize – to begin with the notion of differentness and then define the women as anomalous. There has been no cultural recognition of the fact that women as a group are engulfed in fear and abuse, restricted to inadequate and irrelevant modes of expression, blindly trained towards cultural images of success, and stunted by notions of character and growth that reflect nothing of their reality. Women who have struggled to surmount these growth-inhibiting obstacles but who have been deprived of mutually empathic relationships in their personal worlds and have subsequently been unable to move into growth-fostering social pockets, are defined as anomalies. However, the basic strivings, needs, and goals of the women in this study are similar to those of women who do not come into conflict with the law.

Like Virginia Woolf, the women in this study struggled in hope but often despaired of ever freeing themselves of the effects of their invisible but none the less genuine damage. Woolf's struggle was visible in her writing and her lecturing. The struggle of the women in this study was visible in their declarations of their goodness and their desire to make connections. Woolf's despair was evident in her 'schizophrenia' and her suicide. The despair of the women in this study was evident in their conflicts with the law, their addictions, and their self-mutilation.

The primary source of empowerment for women – mutually empathic relationships – was missing from these women's lives. The sense of empowerment that enables women to make the best of an often disempowering world was unavailable to them.

When women are empowered to assume that they will find growth-fostering pockets in the world, they become fully functional and are able to experience themselves as effective, or able to make an impact on other people. It is also precisely this kind of empowerment that enables women to leave disempowering relationships. Women who are not empowered in this way become vulnerable to persons and situations through which they may achieve a false and transitory sense of power. In some cases, this ephemeral sense of power is achieved through antisocial acts.

In her studies of moral decision making, Gilligan found that moral and social integration went hand in hand, and that both were contingent upon the women's sense of self-worth. As their self-worth increased, the women in her study began to make 'responsible' rather than 'selfish' decisions. Gilligan states that the transition 'requires a conception of self that includes the possibility for doing "the right thing," the ability to see in oneself the potential for being good and therefore worthy of social inclusion.'[2] The transition involves a 'shift in concern from survival to goodness.'[3] In other words, the women who were the subjects of Gilligan's research were increasingly able to see in themselves the potential for being good, and therefore worthy of social inclusion, and so they were increasingly able to make socially responsible decisions. Unlike the male subjects of Kohlberg's study, who moved towards moral individuation,[4] Gilligan's female participants moved towards moral, and thus social, integration.

The fourteen women in the present study also desired social inclusion. The term *inclusion* implies acceptance by other people, and this clearly was a wish of the women in the study, as evidenced by their ultimate willingness to accept responsibility for their actions. Applying the theory of relational development to the material presented by the women, I found that they had a compelling need to experience themselves as effective in their relationships and in the world. The absence of this experience of empowerment, so fundamental to a woman's developing sense of herself precipitated desperate measures among the women. The issue is not simply that the women were unable to develop to their full potential, but that the deficit in their lives was so critical that they were forced to find ways to mimic what they seemed to know, at some basic level, was essential to their psychological survival.

For these women, lawbreaking was an outgrowth of a complex inter-action of relationships, feelings, and situations, of being denied the essential components of empowerment that might have led to a sense of effectiveness in an inherently disempowering world.

TOWARDS AN INTEGRATED UNDERSTANDING

Early in the process of working with the women's stories in order to understand them as a group, it became obvious that it was not useful to simply identify, in some 'objective' way, common elements such as anger or need. Many women in our society are angry or needy but relatively few of those women are incarcerated, so it cannot be concluded from the identification of such common elements that they precipitated lawbreaking (given that our measure of lawbreaking must be the imperfect measure, the judicial process). It cannot be assumed that the similarities reveal anything about the women's motivation for lawbreaking. Indeed, such similarities in content can be misleading, as they could be the product of extraneous factors, such as the types of probes used in the interviewing process, the circumstances that prevailed in the institution, any of a number of factors influencing arrest, or the fact that the women were all subject to some degree of socialization and stereotyped treatment as females. At the same time, however, given that reasonable precautions were taken to avoid eliciting specific responses, the similarities in the women's stories cannot be assumed to be meaningless.

In the same way, it cannot be assumed that differences in the women's stories do not tell us something about their lawbreaking. On the contrary, the differences enlarge our understanding of the complexities of lawbreaking.

As I sorted out the significance of the similarities and differences in the women's stories, it became clear that the solution to the puzzle lay with the women themselves. Each of the women was able to identify the reasons that made sense to her for her conflict with the law or to describe the path that led to it. Arriving at this personal understanding involved assigning meaning to experiences, a process that cannot be separated from the issue of lawbreaking. What one person experiences as deprivation or a threat may seem less significant to another; hence, subjective meaning must be integrated into explanations of lawbreaking, not dismissed as unscientific or rendered invisible through the application of theory or statistical procedures. Indeed, subjective interpretations of experience can direct and integrate understanding. The women's meanings are derived from and shaped by their own backgrounds and are contingent on their economic situation, their race, their ethnicity, and their place in history.[5]

As I studied the subjective views of the women, it became apparent that their lawbreaking was the outcome of a complex process involving the individual in interaction with her social world, both immediate and general. The subjective view is of primary importance precisely because of the complexity of the topic. The distinction between 'poverty' and 'need' serves as a useful example. As Worrall points out, 'poverty' is a social category by which is implied an objective measure of assessment, whereas 'need' is a subjective measure.[6] From the discussion of need in this book, the nature and complexity of the subjective view, and its value to an understanding of lawbreaking, are readily apparent. Distinguishing between 'need' and 'poverty' in criminological studies could lead to an understanding of why women commit far fewer crimes than men despite the fact that they are, on the whole, economically poorer. Examining lawbreaking through the subjective lens of the women's own stories allows both for the incorporation of issues such as race, ethnicity, class, and historical period into an understanding of lawbreaking, and for the clarification of misleading 'objective' facts. Ultimately, the psychological and social rift can be bridged, leading to a clearer understanding of highly complex issues.

Motivation through the Subjective Lens

One issue that was illuminated through the subjective lens was motivation. In the first interview with each woman, the subject of motivation was not pursued directly, and the questioning was sufficiently open-ended that the women could interpret and respond in whatever way they saw fit, naming the factors that they believed were influential in their lawbreaking. None the less, many of the women responded as though they were discussing internal motivation and personal responsibility for breaking the law. When they were asked directly what they felt were the reasons for their law-breaking, they responded in the same vein. This kind of response is not consistent with a sociological view of lawbreaking in which social structures rather than individuals are implicated as causal. The responses that the women gave tended to locate responsibility in the individual. It might be argued that the women truly felt that they were totally responsible, or that they had internalized social values that emphasize individual responsibility. However, during the course of the interviews, it also became clear that they were aware of contributing factors outside themselves.

For these fourteen women, breaking the law amounted to an expression of themselves and their situations; it was an expression of their attempts to acquire a sense of instrumentality or power in their lives. Some of the women stole candy when they were children because they had no money to buy it and they wanted to be like other children, or began to run away from home in an attempt to make their parents stop arguing or fighting. In adolescence, some began to use street drugs or alcohol, or both, to ease the pain created by a family situation and to find comfort in belonging to a group. Other women were trying to live up to internalized familial and social expectations.

It was not the initial intention of any of the women to act out in a way that would hurt anyone; indeed, many took comfort in the fact that they had tried to avoid hurting people. They felt separate from and powerless within society, including its social agencies, institutions, and systems, so their struggle was, essentially, to find ways to empower themselves.

For the women who broke the law on more than one occasion – that is, all the women except Marianne, Arlene, and Lynne – the motivation for the first act was different from the motivation for the most recent act. In other words, their motivation varied with the stage of their lives and their previous history of lawbreaking. The notion of secondary motivation was introduced in Chapter 4, in the discussion about the women who were addicted to drugs. However, multi-tiered motivation was evident in many of the women's stories. As an adolescent, Vicki went along on a 'b & e' 'for something to do.' Later, she set fire to a building to vent the anger that masked her depression and hurt. Connie stole mascara from a store when she was eighteen to 'see if you can get away with it'; later, she cashed a welfare cheque to which she was not 'entitled,' because she needed the money to heat her home; in addition, she was serving a sentence for a crime she committed in order to stay employed and, thus, to ensure a reasonable lifestyle for herself and her children.

For the women who abused drugs, the initial motivation for breaking the law was obscured by a peculiarity of law enforcement. Despite the fact that possession of street drugs is illegal, arrests are so rare that possession is largely overlooked, by drug abusers, as an illegal act. Thus, some of the women initially stated that they had broken the law to support their drug habit, overlooking their primary motivation for the drug abuse itself. The latter, in fact, centred around family or social problems. The secondary motivation for lawbreaking was to alleviate the pain of withdrawal – the women broke the law to support their drug habit. There were other factors contributing to their addiction: They found a sense of shared purpose in their interactions with other addicts, and they developed an extremely busy and exciting lifestyle. The procurement of a steady supply of drugs usually requires work, which, like the effect of the drugs themselves, provides a diversion from the addict's pain. In addition, the women found a measure of satisfaction in developing the skills needed to maintain their habit.

For these women, motivation was a complex aspect of lawbreaking that defied simple definition and that has implications for our understanding of lawbreaking in general. Individual motivation was not exclusive of social factors, but, rather, both were important considerations. The notion of multi-tiered motivation is essential to understanding the evolving cycles of lawbreaking that become the pattern of some women's lives.

WOMEN, MEN, AND GENDER

This study of fourteen women substantiates the need to carry out research exclusively with female lawbreakers. Many of the facts of their lives that form the web of circumstances surrounding their lawbreaking are specific to women: the births, deaths, and care of children; abuse by men; dependence on men or the social system for economic maintenance; and identification with abused mothers. To lump female lawbreakers together with male lawbreakers without regard for these details of their lives, or to include all of these facets of women's lives under the rubric of gender issues, would be to blur the experiences of the two groups and to render conclusions irrelevant. Nor is it appropriate to cloak the women's stories in ideologies that simply may not fit. Their stories must be understood within the social milieu in which they take place.

Morris and Gelsthorpe recently argued that women cannot be studied apart from men or from gender considerations. If we are to study women's oppression, we need to understand men's role in that oppression.[7] However, taking man-made states such as women's oppression into account does not necessarily demand the inclusion of male lawbreakers in a study of women's lawbreaking. Since man-made states and structures are ubiquitous, we need only to expose them and recognize their impact on women. This is possible whether or not men, as such, are included in the study. Gender considerations are implicit in the exposure of man-made states and structures.

The converse is not necessarily true. The study of gender does not necessarily reveal information about men as a sex or women as a sex. Allen suggests that, if crime were considered sex-specific, we could do away with questions that weigh women's criminality against men's, and pose direct questions to explore women's and men's crime.[8] Since sex-specific questions have not been asked in the past, the study of criminality has been no more a study of men's criminality than it has been a study of women's criminality. Moreover, the clear indications of the present research are that women's lawbreaking can best be understood when the focus is on issues specific to women, so it seems reasonable to consider that men's lawbreaking might also be best understood with a similar focus on issues specific to men.

Currie, however, points out that an overemphasis on sex might obscure the 'similarities in the social characteristics of both male and female offenders.'[9] Indeed, there are strong indications that the present study of women contains lessons that might usefully be applied to the study of men's lawbreaking. For example, it may be enlightening to approach men's lawbreaking from the perspective of relational development theory, since society sets the stage for disconnection rather than connection for men as well as women. Our psychology is premised on separation and individuation, which is consistent with social values based on individuality. However, there is a discrepancy between ideology and practice. Separation is the espoused ideology, but support through relationships is often the practice. Thus, we honour men who are 'self-made,' but fail to give full credit to the mentoring systems, the networks, and the wives and families who make men's achievements possible. The practice belies the belief, but we continue to be guided by the fiction of separation and individuation. Men, in particular, are guided by this fiction, many having failed to recognize and come to terms with the discrepancy. Striving to achieve the goals of separation and individuation can create a disjuncture between what is known and felt implicitly and what is practised publicly.[10]

If men, like women, have strong relational needs, a relational theory may help explain both men's and women's lawbreaking. In our society, men face a much stronger imperative than women to pursue the goals of separation and individuation.[11] Perhaps it is not a coincidence that men have a much greater propensity for conflict with the law.

Excluding male lawbreakers from the study of female lawbreakers does not mean that men do not figure heavily into women's conflicts with the law. By exposing the structures and states that oppress women, such studies implicate men. Some of the fathers of the women in this study emerged as influential causal factors as a result of their expectations of themselves, their motives (which were based on the separation model), and their perpetuation of the separation ideology. The violence of some fathers interfered with the women's relationships with their mothers. In some cases, the father's greed, violence, or opportunism was played out on the daughter directly. Some fathers insisted on inculcating their daughters with social values steeped in the rhetoric of individualism. Others seemed to be reacting against situations that prevented their own adherence to the separation–individuation ethic. Those were the men who had been injured and were unable to work, and whose essential dependence on their families and on systems outside themselves was being exposed. In some of those cases, gross abuses followed. It may be that their abuse of others gave the men the sense of separateness or individuality that men normally derive through their position as income-earners. The women's husbands or partners were sometimes abusive as well, or refused to honour their responsibilities towards the women and their children. Other men, too, influenced the events of the women's lives: in some cases, they were employers who demanded support from the women but gave none in return; in others, they were opportunists who preyed on women's vulnerabilities. Exposing these machinations is of central importance to understanding women's conflicts with the law.

TOWARDS APPLYING THIS NEW UNDERSTANDING OF FEMALE
LAWBREAKERS

Of primary importance in understanding women's lawbreaking is the need to reconceptualize it as a struggle on the part of the women to become effective in their personal relationships and in the world, rather than as a wilful perpetration of acts against society. The lack of growth-enhancing relationships in their lives left the women in this study with severe deficits in their capacity to act in the world as if it were a growth-fostering environment. It is imperative that ways be found to facilitate the development in women of the power to act on their own behalf, in legally acceptable ways. This is in sharp contrast to an approach in which the emphasis is on conformity to a society that is experienced by women as disempowering.

It is at this juncture that women as victims of crime and of the social structure intersect with women as perpetrators of lawbreaking activity. The stories told by the women show clearly that the devastating effects of violence against women reach far beyond the actual physical or psychological battering. Violence interfered with the relationships of many of the women and their mothers by depleting the mothers' capacity to relate empathically with their daughters. In Doris's case, violence and other abusive behaviours that had been part of her social milieu became her own mode of expression. Danielle was first a victim of physical abuse, then used violence in self-defence after her many complaints to police were ignored. Men who held financial power over the women victimized them in subtle ways that convinced them they had no choice but to break the law. The pressures inherent in a materialistic and individualistic society created particular problems for underpaid and unsupported women who wanted their children to 'have a childhood' like other children. In Vicki's case, cultural alienation in an oppressed society produced personal disconnections from loved ones, and the associated emotional states overwhelmed her.

Solutions to the issues identified in this study must accommodate both the psychological and the social aspects of women's lives. Some important recommendations for changes in the prison system have already been described in Creating Choices: The Report of the Task Force on Federally Sentenced Women,[12] and Carlen has suggested thought-provoking measures in her Alternatives to Women's Imprisonment.[13] The recommendations that follow have emerged from the specific understandings generated by the present study and include both broad brush-strokes and specific suggestions.

Women must be freed of the burden of victimization, or they will continue to come into conflict with the law. Community agencies must end their isolation from each other and endeavour to work cooperatively for the benefit of women. Continuing efforts must be made by the justice system, social agencies, and educational institutions to expose and eradicate violence against women and children. Agencies such as the Workers' Compensation Board might be alerted to the fact that abusiveness can develop among men who are incapacitated for long periods of time as a result of on-the-job injuries. Continuing efforts must be made by and in cooperation with Aboriginal people to expunge the violence from their lives. Governments must redouble efforts to ensure that women are treated equitably in the workplace. Hospitals and medical professionals in the community and in prisons must become educated about the effects of miscarriage and stillbirth on women, and be prepared to counsel them through their experience of the loss. A valuing of relationships and of the life-giving and life-affirming functions traditionally assigned to women – the nurturing functions – must be woven into the social fabric.

Prison and probation and parole systems must learn from the women in their charge and develop appropriate resources and methods of helping them to become integrated into society. One important resource for working with women in prison is the staff of correctional officers, whose impact, through their day-to-day interactions with them, can be profound.[14] Correctional officers are well placed to have an effect on the women by exercising an ethic of 'power to change' rather than of 'power over.' Research and educational efforts would wisely be spent on the exploration and piloting of projects in which correctional officers can develop new perceptions of their purpose and their method of operation in an institution. By conceptualizing their tasks around a core of empathy, compassion, and the power to effect positive change, the officers as well as the women might become empowered to feel more effective in their worlds. Creative measures are needed to balance security requirements with the needs of the women, all with an awareness that, because the women have learned to mistrust the responses of others, they may initially test the limits and safety of any new approach, particularly an empathic approach.

Another important resource is the women themselves. If an empathic milieu is to be created, the women must be able to act with compassion towards one another. Although, in some prisons, peer support programs have been initiated and have proved to be beneficial as a support to professional counselling,[15] problems in developing an empathic support system are to be expected, because people who have been severely oppressed are sometimes the least understanding of others whose positions mirror their own. In a hierarchical world, the weakest fight among themselves and consciously or inadvertently support those who have power over them, because this seems the safest alternative. If they are encouraged to think of themselves as part of the larger population, women in conflict with the law might find it possible to be more open to connections with a wider range of women. In prison, disputes between women might be resolved through a form of crisis conflict resolution rather than through separation and segregation of the women. Such a process would involve uncovering relational issues and repairing the disjunctures through a mediation process involving empathic connecting. Similarly, responses to self-abuse must be supportive; women must be heard at such times, not isolated. Balancing security issues with women's needs when women self-mutilate is a delicate problem. However, these disparate needs could perhaps be met by transforming a space in the prison into a healing room, where the woman at risk could stay, safely, until she believed that her crisis period had subsided and she felt ready to reintegrate, fully, into the general milieu. Specially briefed peer volunteers could provide a twenty-four-hour vigil for the woman, simply sitting with her and allowing her to talk according to her needs. It would be understood that the volunteer would have the complete and immediate support of correctional officers if necessary.

Essential to the development of programs to foster empowerment would be an assessment of the degree to which the women are able to tolerate empathic relationships. As noted earlier, many women have become suspicious of empathic responses; indeed, their relationships are likely to be highly transitory or chaotic because of a fundamental inability to trust. Clearly, special approaches to building trust must be employed with such women.

One vehicle for the exchange of mutual empathy might be a program in which women are closely coached in empathic responsiveness to their children. (Such a program would be appropriate only for women who are able to tolerate empathic responses.) The very process through which the women learned to respond to their children would involve them in empathic and empowering exchanges with their coaches.

For many of the women in this study, grief was a concealed but highly significant factor. My experience with other women in the prison suggested that the women I interviewed were not exceptional in this regard. Both social service agencies and prisons need to be aware that uncompleted grieving lurks in the background of many women who come into conflict with the law. The loss of children through miscarriage, stillbirth, adoption, or death must be dealt with directly as soon as the women feel safe enough to grieve. It is also important for counsellors to explore the ways in which such losses have influenced the women's own developmental processes. Understanding that some women may not feel safe revealing their grief in prison, even in the privacy of counselling sessions, authorities must ensure that appropriate assistance will be available to them in the community when they need it.

When the focus is on treatment for drug addiction, it is important to find ways to fill the huge void that the loss of the habit leaves in the addict's life. As Penny, a heroin addict, said, 'Straightening out and having no job is just waiting for relapse.' Given the nature of the drug addict's lifestyle, the usual types of jobs available to women who are relatively uneducated are hardly a solution, because they underemploy the rather sophisticated skills these women have developed through living by their wits. If these skills cannot be used, or if substitutes cannot be found, boredom will surely set in and the cycle will repeat itself. Exposing motivational tiers is also important in working with women who are drug addicted so that areas of vulnerability can be identified and appropriate coping mechanisms developed.

In a survey conducted by the Task Force on Federally Sentenced Women, many of the women who were substance abusers said that the treatment programs offered in the prisons did not reflect their experiences.[16] Hence, prison treatment programs might usefully be revamped to take into account the women's acquired skills, and to build on them. Such programs would incorporate nonjudgmental discussions about the women's experiences of drug acquisition; the women's skills would be identified and isolated; and the emphasis would gradually be shifted from the drug use to the skills. The objective of such programs would be to shift the association between feelings of euphoria and the drug to an association between feelings of euphoria and the skills and aptitudes that were involved in acquiring the drug, such as resourcefulness, planning, organization, time management, knowledge of bodily responses, and an ability to 'read' other people's intentions and responses. A final and essential part of such programs would be the application of these skills to socially acceptable situations, creating the opportunity for women to experience themselves as effective in socially acceptable ways.

Similarly, anger in women must not be feared but understood. Correctional programs currently recognize that inmates' anger must be addressed, but are usually directed strictly at managing the anger.[17] This approach suggests that anger is unrelated to other emotions. The experiences of the women in this study, however, support Caplan's conception of anger as a secondary emotion.[18] Therefore, a more useful path might be to encourage women, in a safe setting, to 'move into' their anger in order to identify the underlying emotions that ignite the sequence of reactions leading to potentially explosive behaviour.

Programs must be developed with an awareness that women are relational beings. If program designers fail to understand that women do not live in isolation from other people, their programs are likely to resolve nothing. For about three years, in her late teens, Penny took part in a government-sponsored program that involved supplying heroin addicts with methadone. Although her participation kept her off heroin for that period, it did not prevent her from breaking the law. She continued to break the law in order to supply heroin to her 'boyfriend,' who wasn't eligible for the methadone program.

The importance of understanding that women do not live in isolation is evident on a larger scale. One of the segments of the population of female lawbreakers that are most difficult to reach includes women like Penny, who accumulate multiple but not lengthy sentences. Penny is one of many so-called career prisoners, who are incarcerated on a revolving-door basis throughout their lifetime. They tend to be held in the provincial prisons for short periods of time, so they rarely benefit from treatment programs that require time for completion and integration. These women are the truly difficult to reach because they are continually moving between the community and the prison. Their movement necessitates more comprehensive community links with the prisons to provide continuity of relationships, support, and treatment.

Finally, it is of utmost importance that counselling and therapy with female lawbreakers be informed by a feminist rather than a masculinist perspective on women's position in society. Women's treatment must emerge from women's knowledge and experiences of the world and themselves. As discussed earlier, there is no single, universal 'woman's experience'; there are women's experiences. This means that therapy must begin with each woman's subjective view; strict ideological frameworks must be suspended and the focus must be on understanding the client's perception of herself and her situation. This approach can challenge any therapist's strongly held belief system. However, it is important to move, unafraid, into an understanding of women's experiences, even when that understanding seems to contradict a feminist understanding. This movement inward will be the strength of the therapy and will provide the foundation for the development of the woman's own increasing understanding of her position in the social structure. A rigid template for therapy may prevent the therapist from hearing, for example, that, in her deprived-child state, Bonnie experienced the sexual abuse at the hands of her uncles as pleasurable and as her only source of 'affection' during that particular period of her life. Adopting a rigid stance as to what a child or a woman must feel preempts hearing, connection, a full understanding of the individual experience, therapeutic movement, healing, and empowerment.

RESEARCH DIRECTIONS

One of the benefits of providing a forum for people to speak is the creation of a fertile ground for expanding exploration. The present study yielded a rich web of possibilities for research. Among them are the following:

- An exploration of the impact of losses such as stillbirth and miscarriage on the developmental process of teenage mothers.
- A study of male lawbreakers through the lens of relational development theory, informed by a feminist understanding of men's place in the social structure.
- A study of correctional officers' attitudes towards power.
- A pilot study of correctional officers' training in and practice of an ethic of 'power to effect change.'
- A study of families in which the primary income-earner has been unemployed and remains unemployable, to determine the risk of abuse as an outcome of the situation; this must be a gendered study that asks sex-specific questions of male and female income-earners.
  It might, in fact, be useful to explore the impact of men's employment patterns on women's lawbreaking in general. Several studies might emerge, including an exploration of the impact of the relational breakdowns that can occur when men become abusive as a result of work-related injury and subsequent loss of employment.
- Career counsellors might be engaged to carry out aptitude and interest assessments on women in prison, both as a way of helping them find their direction and as a concrete and validating interaction.
- An exploration of the emotions and processes underlying female lawbreakers' anger.
- Research to expand on the 'good touch, bad touch' education that children currently receive, to determine whether it is effective, in view of the fact that children who are at the highest risk for victimization may be predisposed to experience sexual abuse that is physically pain-free as a form of caring; this applies to almost any child before the age at which social boundaries are understood.
- Research that conceptualizes motivation as fluid and evolving, to bridge the gap between the study of juvenile delinquency and the study of adult lawbreaking.
- It may be useful to explore whether there is any significance in the following: (1) that all the Black women in this study identified need as

the reason for their conflict with the law, and (2) that the two women who were adopted identified anger as the reason.

Finally, in keeping with the spirit of this book, we must ask women who were once lawbreakers but have since become law-abiding what, in their view, helped them to change.

Research 'Design'

Lincoln and Guba point out that it is paradoxical to 'design' a study in which exploration is the fundamental characteristic.[1] Exploration demands an 'openness to surprise,' which precludes rigid design elements.[2] The 'design,' then, must emerge from the research. I have incorporated into the design of this study Hunt's approach, which emphasizes 'reflexivity, responsiveness and reciprocality,'[3] combining the elements of awareness and acknowledgment of one's own experience, attitudes, and intentions with a sensitivity to the experience of the participant, and recognizing a mutuality of benefit for the researcher and the participants.[4]

Early on, it became evident that there would be three phases to the research – an immersion phase, an acquisition phase, and a synthesis and analysis phase.[5] The immersion phase was a period of exploration and discovery. It included self-examination, focusing on my own perspective on research, lawbreaking, and lawbreakers; resource interviews with two women, one an inmate and one a former inmate; a review of the literature; and participant observation in the prison. The process of self-examination included a confrontation with my own and my colleagues' experiences of lawbreaking. Each one of us could recount instances of breaking the law – by speeding, incurring parking fines, and so on. Although it is tempting to say that we are not unlike women who are imprisoned and that the real difference lies in the fact that only particular groups of women and men become victims of the justice system, such an evaluation trivializes the seriousness of the women's lawbreaking and denies that, for some, the circumstances are much more grave – so grave that they have to resort to desperate measures.

The acquisition phase included the selection of the participants, and the interviews. Certain principles were fundamental to the research: (1) the

hierarchical nature of the interview situation was recognized and levelled
to the extent that that was possible and desirable; (2) the women were
fully informed of the value of their contribution, so that they could experience their participation as meaningful; (3) the research process was
meant to provide an opportunity for self-discovery or catharsis, as well as
an opportunity to help other women; and (4) there was a reciprocality
between the interviewer and the participants, in that the latter were provided with feedback.[6]

To be consistent with an emergent design, the phase in which sense is
made of the material – in this case, the synthesis and analysis phase – must
also be exploratory and open to discovery. Although procedures must be
followed consistently, the rules of analysis need not be formally described
until the end of the analysis.[7] In a study of this nature, the work of understanding stories collectively and locating the points of confluence while
honouring and allowing for the richness of each woman's meanings and
experiences is a task that requires sensitivity to the possibility of distortion.
Kirby and McKenna identify two important components in the process of
analysis: intersubjectivity, or the recognition that the participants' contributions are of equal value, and a critical reflection on the social context
of the participants' lives. Both of these components are necessary to ensure
that the words and experiences of the participants are heard and affirmed,
while at the same time 'the structures that influence the actualities of their
lives' are considered.[8]

The concept of analysis – the usual approach to a body of research
material – implies a separation into parts. Analysing the interview material
in the absence of any real understanding of the women as whole persons
would have amounted to a fragmentation, and a repetition of the error of
studies that have focused on one aspect or another of women's lawbreaking and criminality. It became evident, in my initial encounter with the
material, that, before I could conduct a relevant analysis, I would have to
transfer my sense of each woman as a whole person to the printed page.
Therefore, before proceeding with the analysis, which would necessarily
fragment the women's stories, I pieced together the events of the women's
lives from the interview material, and created a whole story of each woman's life. I then had a context for each woman within which to understand
each emergent theme.

In the next step of the synthesis and analysis phase, I isolated each
woman's stated reason for breaking the law and reconstructed the developmental process of her conflict with the law by piecing together relevant
details from her story. Thus, the resultant four themes and the structure

of the presentation of the results emerged from the women's statements about their reasons for their conflict with the law. As I worked through the material in this way, it further became evident that two implicit themes existed in the women's stories which were common to all of them.

Establishing Trustworthiness

An argument that is often levelled against qualitative studies – studies based on depth rather than breadth – is that the small numbers of participants and the use of interview material without control or comparison groups render such studies invalid or unreliable. Lincoln and Guba, however, have identified four characteristics on the basis of which qualitative studies can be evaluated: credibility, transferability, dependability, and confirmability.[1]

Credibility is the 'truth value' of a study, or the extent to which the realities of the individuals studied are represented. A study gains credibility through prolonged engagement with those studied, persistent observation, triangulation, and approval of the reconstructions of the participants' realities by the participants themselves. My work with dozens of women in the prison and my observation of them in their day-to-day routines thus lent credibility to the study. In addition, as a first step in developing an understanding of the stories of the women as a group, I pieced together the events of the women's lives from the interview material, and created a whole story of each woman's life. The reconstructed stories of six of the participants were completed while the women (and I) were still in the institution, and I gave these to the six women to read. The purpose of this 'member check' is to determine whether the reconstruction of the material is recognizable as an adequate representation of each woman's own reality.[2] The women were asked for their comments and for their views as to whether anything should be changed, omitted, or added. One woman wanted to make an addition, and it was made. Comments included 'good,' 'excellent,' 'like me talking to me,' 'accurate,' 'weird, because I've had such a long life and this is so short,' 'weird, reading the story, knowing it all happened to me.' One woman said, 'I can't believe I had so much pain and sadness inside me. I was like a volcano ready to erupt and I guess I did.'

As another form of member check, I had a psychologist and a psychometrist who were experienced with the population of women in prison read the women's stories and verify their credibility, based on the stories they themselves had heard from women in the course of their experience in the prison system.

There are other ways of establishing the credibility of a qualitative study. Credibility is demonstrated by one's 'openness to surprise,'[3] something that was evident in the shift that I experienced in my understanding of women's lawbreaking. I tested this development by constructing a model of my understanding at the beginning of the study, by keeping a journal, and by comparing my understanding when the study was completed with my initial understanding. Repetition of the material during the course of the interviews also confirms credibility.[4] I had structured the research to include four interviews with each woman over a period of four weeks. This meant that if stories had been fabricated as we talked, the details would likely have been forgotten between interviews. Therefore, details repeated spontaneously at intervals could be taken as an indication of veracity.

Of course, it is always possible that research participants might be practised in fabrication and might lie to invalidate the research, in which case repetition might be planned. However, defences against this eventuality were implicit in the research: the open-ended questions provided opportunities not only for fabrication but also for contradiction; details of stories that did give pause were integrated cautiously into the research material; and the multiple-interview format provided the opportunity to ask questions to confirm or disconfirm statements.

Lincoln and Guba's second criterion for assessing qualitative studies is transferability.[5] The assessment of transferability is the task of the person interested in applying the research in new contexts, because only he or she knows the new context. The responsibility of the researcher is to supply a 'thick description,' by which the person applying the research can judge the relevance and usefulness of the material to a new application and, in this way, assess transferability. It is for this reason that the present study recounts the women's stories in rich detail.

The third criterion for assessment is dependability, which can be achieved through techniques such as triangulation.[6] In this research, comments made by inmates and recorded throughout my extended period of participant observation provided spontaneous and continual affirmations of the kinds of issues and themes that emerged from the interview material.[7]

Confirmability of the research material, Lincoln and Guba's final cri-terion of assessment, was also achieved through my day-to-day observations of the women in the prison, which I recorded in a journal. Under the criterion of confirmability, the characteristics of the material, not the objectivity of the researcher, are at issue.[8] Objectivity is a fundamental principle of research in the natural sciences that has been adopted by the social sciences. A discussion of objectivity is included in the text.

Research participants often behave differently in an interview situation than in a more natural setting.[9] Therefore, as another part of the validation process of the research, I compared my observations of the participants in the more 'natural' setting of the institution with my experiences of them in the interview situation.

Notes

1 Lawbreaking is the act of breaking rules. It is not my task in this book to debate the relevance of the established rules. (It is accepted that the rules and procedures for enforcing them have been created by a patriarchal system that favours particular groups, often to the detriment of women.) Rather, the purpose is to explore the women's reasons for breaking these man-made rules, since this is the system in which we all live, and with which most women and men – happily or otherwise – apparently comply.

2 In her work on mental illness, Dorothy Smith (1986) postulated that a particular set of documentary procedures led to the creation of the label *mental illness*. The acquisition of the label *criminal* similarly involves procedures rooted in a textual, or documentary, reality. Thus, many people commit acts that contravene, or 'break,' the law; relatively few become 'criminals.' The process of becoming a 'criminal' involves police interpretation of the law in a given situation, coupled with documentation, as well as judicial interpretation and conviction (documentation). These interpretations occur within the framework of government legislation. According to these distinctions, the women I interviewed are both lawbreakers and criminals. None the less, it is not the process of becoming a criminal but the process of lawbreaking – breaking rules – that is the concern of this book. In references to the existing literature throughout this book, however, the terms *crime* and *criminal* appear as they are commonly used in the literature.

3 Smith (1986) notes that women have systematically been excluded from owning knowledge on any level, even when that knowledge is of themselves.

4 The strategy to determine sample completion followed what Lincoln and Guba (1985) called 'maximum variation sampling,' so that information could be obtained from the widest range of participants possible. To avoid over- or underrepresentation of particular age groups or offences, an outline of the distribution of ages and offences for the province was obtained from the Ministry of Correctional Services and used as a guideline for selection. Information was not available for race and ethnic group.
5 LaPrairie, 1987
6 This form of interviewing follows Spradley's (1979) notion of a 'grand tour' question designed to draw from the participants' 'expert' knowledge of their own experiences.
7 Harding, in Harding, 1987
8 Du Bois, 1983; Lincoln & Guba, 1985; Sullivan, 1984
9 Hunt, 1992:118
10 Jaggar, 1977:254
11 Hunt, 1992:114
12 Wine, 1983
13 Sherif, 1987
14 Although, in the present study, the subjective understanding of the women interviewed provided the basic material, the study cannot be considered strictly phenomenological. An interpretive element – that is, my own understanding and interpretation of the material acquired through read-

ing, resource interviews, and participant observation – was also an important component of the research. As Kirby and McKenna (1989) suggest, 'the act of interpretation underlies the entire research process' (p. 23). Moreover, my understanding and interpretation were informed by my experience as a counsellor to dozens of women in the prison.
  None the less, it is important to be clear about the role of interpretation in this research. My first priority was to let the women speak; my second priority was to avoid distorting their words. In order to honour the second priority, I have stayed very close to the women's words when making my interpretations. Many direct and somewhat lengthy quotations are included in this document so that readers may judge for themselves whether or not my interpretations are free of distortion.
15 Hunt, 1987
16 Gilligan, 1982
17 See, for example, J.B. Miller, 1984; 1986; Surrey, 1984, 1990; Kaplan, 1983; Jordan, 1986; and other titles in the Stone Center Working Papers Series.
18 Surrey, 1990:3
19 Bernardez, 1987:5
20 J.B. Miller, 1988
21 Kaplan, 1991:6
22 Shaw et al. (1991) point out the incomplete nature of file informa-

tion in their profile of women
sentenced under federal law.

CHAPTER TWO

1 Leahey, 1987
2 Smart, 1976
3 According to Merton's strain
theory, (1938, 1975), criminality
is a product of accepting cultural
goals of success while having limited opportunity for achieving
that success. Merton's idea is that
society exerts pressure on certain
individuals by denying them
opportunities and thereby forcing
them into deviant rather than
conforming behaviour. For a feminist critique of Merton's strain
theory, see Naffine, 1987.
4 Becker (1963) postulated that
most people commit deviant acts,
but only those people to whom
the label *deviant* is applied rede-
fine their identities and think of
themselves as deviants. For feminist critiques of Becker's labelling
theory, see Leonard, 1982, and
Naffine, 1987.
5 Sutherland and Cressey, 1966.
For a feminist critique of the
theory of differential association,
see Heidensohn, 1985, and Naffine, 1987.
6 Hirschi, 1969. For feminist critiques of control theory, see A.
Morris, 1987, and Naffine, 1987.
7 Lombroso & Ferrero, 1895/1959
8 Freud, 1965
9 Abrahamsen, 1960

10 Thomas, 1923
11 Glueck & Glueck, 1934:322, 299
12 Parsons, 1949
13 Pollak, 1950
14 Konopka, 1966
15 Cowie, Cowie, & Slater, 1968
16 Cowie, Cowie, & Slater,
1968:174
17 Dalton, 1961
18 L.O. Pike (*History of Crime in
England* [London: Smith & Elder,
1876]), cited in Heidensohn,
1985; Bishop, 1931; Adler, 1975
19 Simon, 1975
20 Heidensohn, 1968
21 Klein, 1973
22 Hoffman-Bustamente, 1973
23 Parsons, 1949
24 Smart, 1976
25 Smart, 1976
26 Simpson, 1989
27 L.O. Pike (*History of Crime in
England*, 1876), cited in Heidensohn, 1985; Bishop, 1931; Pollak,
1950
28 Adler, 1975
29 Simon, 1975
30 Worrall, 1990:3
31 See Mukherjee & Fitzgerald,
1981; Steffensmeier, 1981; Johnson, 1987; Naffine, 1987.
32 See Klein & Kress, 1976; Terry,
1979; Giordano, Kerbel, and
Dudley, 1981; Gora, 1982; Johnson, 1987.
33 See Austin, 1982; Box & Hale,
1983.
34 Chesney-Lind, 1980
35 James & Thornton, 1980
36 Crites, 1976; Fox & Hartnagel,

1979; Morris & Gelsthorpe, 1981; Naffine, 1987; Daly & Chesney-Lind, 1988
37 Smart, 1976
38 Naffine, 1981
39 For example, see Currie, 1986; Gelsthorpe & Morris, 1990; A. Morris, 1987; Morris & Gelsthorpe, 1991; and Naffine, 1987.
40 Smart, 1976
41 Valverde, 1991
42 Chesler, 1972
43 Brownmiller, 1975
44 For analyses of the social structure, see Carlen, 1985, 1988; Adelberg & Currie, 1987; Bardsley, 1987.
45 Rice, 1990
46 Windschuttle, 1981:37
47 Carlen, 1988
48 Carlen, 1988:70
49 Carlen, 1988:70
50 Mathews, 1987
51 Worrall, 1990
52 See Gordon, 1988.
53 Widom, 1981:44

CHAPTER THREE

1 Rose's drug use was probably not the official reason for the termination of her 'mothers' allowance.' The legislation that regulates social assistance in the province in which she lived forbids discrimination on the basis of lifestyle. It is more likely that there was a lapse in her custody of the children, which would have resulted in the termination of Family Benefits; alternatively, there may have been some question regarding her earnings.
2 Cressey & Ward, 1969; Prins, 1982: Gabor, 1986
3 Adelberg & Currie, 1987
4 See articles by Shoalts (1991) and Vienneau (1991).
5 Carlen, 1988:4
6 Gabor, 1986:46
7 Carlen, 1988
8 Caplan, 1989:80
9 Caplan, 1989:80
10 Turner, 1985
11 Turner, 1985

CHAPTER FOUR

1 J.B. Miller, 1988:5
2 J.B. Miller, 1988:7
3 See, for example, Bass & Davis, 1988; Courtois, 1988; and Rivera, 1991.
4 Zeanah, 1989
5 Lewis, 1976, used this term to describe women's experiences of stillbirth and miscarriage.
6 Leon, 1986:315
7 Courtois, 1988
8 Heney (1990) describes self-injurious behaviour as a way of coping with the intense anxiety and self-blame that she believes is an outcome of sexual abuse in childhood.
9 Coleman & Colgan, 1986
10 Cohen (1986) made this determination in a psychosocial study of 663 drug addicts.

11 J.B. Miller, 1988
12 Stiver, 1990
13 Surrey, 1985
14 Jordan, 1991a
15 Coleman & Colgan, 1986
16 Stiver, 1990
17 Brown, 1988; Caplan, 1989
18 J.B. Miller, 1988
19 Stiver, 1990
20 Johnson, Marcos, & Bahr, 1987
21 Johnson, Marcos, & Bahr, 1987:335
22 Stiver, 1990:3
23 Brown, 1988
24 Yalom, 1980

CHAPTER FIVE

1 Caplan, 1989:25
2 Tavris, 1989
3 Tavris, 1989
4 Bernardez, 1987:6
5 Canada, 1990a
6 LaPrairie, 1987:133
7 Silman, 1987; York, 1989
8 LaPrairie, 1987
9 Tavris, 1989
10 Browne, 1987
11 Walker, 1989
12 J.B. Miller, 1988:5
13 Walker, 1989:7
14 In their study of federally sentenced women, Shaw et al. (1991) point out that a long sentence cannot be assumed to imply that the woman in question is dangerous and a risk to society.
15 Walker, 1989
16 Browne, 1987
17 Armstrong, 1983

18 A listing of the symptoms of Posttraumatic Stress Disorder can be found in the *DSM-IV*, published by the American Psychiatric Association, 1994.
19 Walker, 1989:48
20 Walker, 1989:48
21 Brant, 1990:535
22 Bernardez, 1977, 1987
23 Naffine, 1987:74
24 Brant, 1990

CHAPTER SIX

1 J.B. Miller, 1988:8
2 Lewis, 1976:620
3 Leon, 1986
4 Zeanah, 1989:468
5 Lewis & Page, 1978:240
6 Bandura, 1977
7 Korbin, 1986
8 J.B. Miller, 1988
9 Caplan, 1989
10 Lewis, 1976
11 Korbin, 1986:336
12 Bakan, 1971; Steele & Pollock, 1974; Kertzman, 1980
13 Melnick & Hurley, 1969; Wiehe, 1985

CHAPTER SEVEN

1 Naffine, 1987
2 Relationships were also found to be of importance to the women incarcerated in the federal system who were interviewed by the Task Force on Federally Sentenced Women in the late 1980s (see Canada, 1990). Eaton (1993)

found that reciprocality in relationships was a pivotal feature of
change in the women she interviewed for *Women after Prison.*
3 R. Morris, 1964; Merton, 1938
4 J.B. Miller, 1988:7
5 Jordan, 1985:9
6 Gilligan, 1982:126
7 Stiver, 1990
8 J.B. Miller, 1982:2
9 Jordan, 1985
10 J.B. Miller, 1988:4
11 Ross & Fabiano, 1985
12 Jordan, 1985:3
13 Surrey, 1984
14 Ross & Fabiano, 1985

CHAPTER EIGHT

1 A. Miller, 1986:318
2 Gilligan, 1982:78
3 Gilligan, 1982:109
4 Kohlberg, 1981
5 A number of books and studies
have identified common factors
and common emotional states in
the lives of female lawbreakers,
similar to those identified in this
research. (See, for example, Adelberg & Currie, 1987; Bardsley,
1987; Carlen, 1985; and the
reports of Shaw et al., 1990,
1991.) In the absence of an analysis in these works of what the
identified common events and
states meant to the women themselves, and in view of the methodological problem inherent in
attaching significance to them, the
identified similarities mean little

in terms of explaining women's
lawbreaking. For example, many,
but not all, female lawbreakers
have been sexually abused. Conversely, many women have been
sexually abused but few are lawbreakers. How, then, do we know
whether, why, and how sexual
abuse is linked to lawbreaking?
We find out only by moving
more deeply into the women's
stories, to uncover their meanings
and understandings. Moreover, it
is only with an understanding of
the underlying reasons for wom-
en's lawbreaking that appropriate
approaches can be devised to
assist the women in their integration into society.
6 Worrall, 1990
7 Morris & Gelsthorpe, 1991
8 Allen, 1989
9 Currie, 1986
10 At least one story has been writ-
ten in which the tension between
separation and connection is pivotal to a man's lawbreaking:
Square John (Webber & Mc-
Gilvary, 1988) chronicles the
story of Tony McGilvary, a con
turned good guy.
11 Although it is true that separation
and individuation are goals more
commonly expected of men than
of women, women are more
likely to be pathologized precisely
because they are oriented towards
relationships rather than towards
separation.
12 Canada, 1990

13 Carlen, 1990
14 In *Creating Choices* (Canada, 1990a), some of the current staffing issues in the federal correctional system are described. In the report, the movement towards an *integration* of 'control, support, and assistance' as opposed to an emphasis on either security or programs is noted. It is stated that federally sentenced women interviewed for the report felt they needed support rather than security.
15 Kendall, 1993
16 Canada, 1990a
17 Kendall, 1993
18 Caplan, 1989

APPENDIX A

1 Lincoln & Guba, 1985
2 Hunt, 1992
3 Hunt, 1992
4 A sensitivity to the people whose experiences and reflections are being studied, and a valuing and preservation of the richness of their situation, are also important elements of this study, and are consistent with the approach taken by Berg (1989) and Lincoln and Guba (1985).
5 The phases of research are similar to those described by Douglass and Moustakas (1985), who labelled their phases immersion, acquisition, and realization. I borrowed the labels for the first two phases and created a more fitting label for my third phase – synthesis and analysis. Although labelled as discrete phases the reality of my research experience was that some aspects of the immersion phase continued throughout the acquisition phase, while the synthesis and analysis phase began during the acquisition phase.
6 Oakley, 1981; Reinharz, 1983; Hunt, 1992
7 Lincoln & Guba, 1985
8 Kiby & McKenna, 1989:130

APPENDIX B

1 These terms, as well as the term *establishing trustworthiness*, are borrowed from Lincoln and Guba (1985).
2 Lincoln and Guba (1985) use the term *member check*.
3 Hunt, 1992:44
4 Taylor & Bogdan, 1984
5 Transferability is the couterpart of generalizability in quantitative research. Generalizability refers to the extent to which the research findings can be applied to the larger population of which the research subjects are one sample.
6 Lincoln and Guba (1985) argue that replicability, the criterion determining the reliability of a quantitative study, 'can be determined only within a given framework – and that framework itself is a construction, not an inevitable and unchanging part of reality' (p. 299). Thus, they opt for a

broader concept, dependability. One of the methods of determining dependability is through triangulation; an example of triangulation is the use of two or more methods of information-gathering (Berg, 1989; Denzin, 1970). Berg describes triangulation as the use of different methods in one research project, each with 'different line of sight directed toward the same point' (p. 4). Triangulation is often thought of as a way of obtaining a deeper and clearer understanding of the setting and people being studied, while limiting researcher bias (Taylor & Bogdan, 1984). In conducting this research, I used participant observation primarily to validate the material gathered in the formal interviews.

7 Taylor and Bogdan (1984) describe participant observation as 'research that involves social interaction between the researcher and informants in the milieu of the latter, during which data are systematically and unobtrusively collected' (p. 15).

8 Lincoln & Guba, 1985.

9 Reinharz, 1983; Taylor & Bogdan, 1984

Bibliography

Abrahamsen, David. (1960). *The psychology of crime.* New York: John Wiley and Sons.

Adelberg, Ellen, and Currie, Claudia (Eds.). (1987). *Too few to count: Canadian women in conflict with the law.* Vancouver: Press Gang.

Adler, Freda. (1975). *Sisters in crime: The new female criminal.* New York: McGraw-Hill.

Allen, Judith. (1989). Men, crime and criminology: Recasting the questions. *International Journal of the Sociology of Law, 17,* 19–39.

American Psychiatric Association. (1994). *Diagnostic and statistical manual of mental disorders* (4th ed., rev.). Washington, DC: American Psychiatric Association.

Anyon, Jean. (1982, January). *Accommodation, resistance, and female gender.* Paper presented at the International Sociology of Education Conference, Birmingham, England.

Armstrong, Louise. (1983). *The home front: Notes from the family war zone.* New York: McGraw-Hill.

Austin, Roy. (1982). Women's liberation and increases in minor, major, and occupational offences. *Criminology, 20,* 407–30.

Bakan, David. (1971). *Slaughter of the innocents.* San Francisco: Jossey-Bass.

Bandura, Albert. (1977). *Social learning theory.* Englewood Cliffs, NJ: Prentice-Hall.

Bandura, Albert. (1979). The social learning perspective: Mechanisms of aggression. In Hans Toch (Ed.), *Psychology of crime and criminal justice.* New York: Holt, Rinehart and Winston.

Bardsley, Barney. (1987). *Flowers in hell: An investigation into women and crime.* London: Pandora.

Bass, Ellen, & Davis, Laura. (1988). *The courage to heal: A guide for women survivors of child sexual abuse.* New York: Harper & Row.

Becker, H. (1963). *Outsiders: Studies in the sociology of deviance*. New York: Free Press.

Berg, B.L. (1989). *Qualitative research methods for the social sciences*. Needham Heights, MA: Allyn and Bacon.

Bernardez, Teresa. (1977, May). *Women and anger: Conflicts with aggression in contemporary women*. Paper presented at the Annual Meeting of the American Psychiatric Association, Toronto, ON.

Bernardez, Teresa. (1987). *Women and anger: Cultural prohibitions and the feminine ideal. Work in progress*. Stone Center Working Papers Series. Wellesley, MA: Stone Center.

Bishop, Cecil. (1931). *Women and crime*. London: Chatto and Windus.

Box, Stephen, & Hale, Chris. (1983). Liberation and female criminality in England and Wales. *British Journal of Criminology, 23* (35), 35–49.

Brant, Clare. (1990). Native ethics and rules of behaviour. *Canadian Journal of Psychiatry, 35* (August), 534–39.

Broverman, I., Broverman, D., Clarkson, F., Rosenkrantz, P., & Vogel, S. (1970). Sex-role stereotypes and clinical judgements of mental health. *Journal of Consulting and Clinical Psychology, 34*, 1–7.

Brown, Stephanie. (1988). *Treating adult children of alcoholics: A developmental perspective*. New York: John Wiley & Sons.

Browne, Angela. (1987). *When battered women kill*. New York: Free Press.

Brownmiller, Susan. (1975). *Against our will: Men, women, and rape*. New York: Bantam.

Campbell, Anne. (1981). *Girl delinquents*. Oxford, UK: Basil Blackwell.

Canada. (1990). *Creating choices: The report of the Task Force on Federally Sentenced Women*. Ottawa: Ministry of the Solicitor General of Canada.

Caplan, Paula J. (1981). *Between women: Lowering the barriers*. Toronto: Personal Library.

Caplan, Paula J. (1989). *Don't blame mother: Mending the mother–daughter relationship*. New York: Harper & Row.

Carlen, Pat. (1985). *Criminal women: Some autobiographical accounts*. Cambridge, UK: Polity Press.

Carlen, Pat. (1988). *Women, crime, and poverty*. Milton Keynes, England: Open University Press.

Carlen, Pat. (1990). *Alternatives to women's imprisonment*. Milton Keynes, England: Open University Press.

Chaplin, J. (1975). *Dictionary of psychology*. New York: Dell.

Chesler, Phyllis. (1972). *Women and madness*. New York: Avon Books.

Chesney-Lind, Meda. (1980). Re-discovering Lilith: Misogyny and the 'new' female criminal. In S. Griffiths & A. Nance (Eds.), *The female offender: Se-*

lected papers from an international symposium. Burnaby, BC: Criminology Centre, Simon Fraser University.

Chesney-Lind, Meda. (1989). Girls' crime and woman's place: Toward a feminist model of female delinquency. *Crime and Delinquency, 35* (1), 5–29.

Cohen, Arie. (1986). A psychosocial typology of drug addicts and implications for treatment. *International Journal of the Addictions, 21,* 147–54.

Coleman, Eli, & Colgan, Phillip. (1986). Boundary inadequacy in drug dependent families. *Journal of Psychoactive Drugs, 18,* 21–30.

Cooper, S.D. (1987). The evolution of the federal women's prison. In E. Adelberg & C. Currie (Eds.), *Too few to count: Canadian women in conflict with the law*. Vancouver: Press Gang.

Courtois, Christine. (1988). *Healing the incest wound: Adult survivors in therapy*. New York: W.W. Norton.

Cowie, John, Cowie, Valerie, & Slater, Eliot. (1968). *Delinquency in girls*. London: Heinemann.

Coyner, Sandra. (1986). The ideas of mainstreaming: Women's studies and the disciplines. *Frontiers, 8*(3), 87–95.

Cressey, Donald, & Ward, David (Eds.). (1969). *Delinquency, crime, and social process*. New York: Harper & Row.

Crites, L. (Ed.). (1976). *The female offender*. Lexington, MA: Lexington Books.

Currie, Dawn. (1986). Female criminality: A crisis in feminist theory. In Brian D. MacLean (Ed.), *The political economy of crime*. Scarborough, ON: Prentice-Hall Canada.

Dalton, Katharina. (1961). Menstruation and crime. *British Medical Journal, 2,* 1752–3.

Daly, Kathleen, & Chesney-Lind, Meda. (1988). Feminism and criminology. *Justice Quarterly, 5,* 497–538.

Denzin, N.K. (1970). *The research act*. Chicago: Aldine.

Douglass, B., & Moustakas, C. (1985). Heuristic inquiry: The internal search to know. *Journal of Humanistic Psychology, 25* (3), 39–55.

Downes, David, & Rock, Paul. (1988). *Understanding deviance: A guide to the sociology of crime and rule breaking*. Oxford, UK: Clarendon Press.

Du Bois, B. (1983). Passionate scholarship: Notes on values, knowing and method in feminist social science. In G. Bowles & R.D. Klein (Eds.), *Theories of women's studies*. New York: Routledge.

Eaton, Mary. (1993). *Women after prison*. Buckingham, England: Open University Press.

Ellis, D., & Austin, P. (1971). Menstruation and aggressive behavior in a correctional center for women. *Journal of Criminal Law, Criminology, and Police Science, 62,* 388–95.

Fausto-Stirling, Anne. (1985). *Myths of gender. Biological theories about men and women*. New York: Basic Books.

Feldman, David. (1969). Psychoanalysis and crime. In Donald Cressey & David Ward (Eds.), *Delinquency, crime, and social process*. New York: Harper & Row.

Fox, John, & Hartnagel, Timothy. (1979). Changing social roles and female crime in Canada: A time series analysis. *Canadian Review of Sociology and Anthropology, 16*, 96–104.

Foxe, Arthur. (1948). *Studies in criminology*. Nervous and Mental Disease Monographs no. 76. New York: Nervous and Mental Disease Monographs.

Franken, Robert. (1982). *Human motivation*. Monterey, CA: Brooks/Cole.

Freud, Sigmund. (1965). *New introductory lectures* (James Strachey, Ed. and Trans.). New York: Norton.

Gabor, Thomas. (1986). *The prediction of criminal behaviour: Statistical approaches*. Toronto: University of Toronto Press.

Gavigan, Shelley. (1987). Women's crime: New perspectives and old theories. In E. Adelberg and C. Currie (Eds.), *Too few to count: Canadian women in conflict with the law*. Vancouver, BC: Press Gang.

Gelsthorpe, Loraine. (1989). *Sexism and the female offender: An organizational Analysis*. Hants, England: Gower.

Gelsthorpe, Loraine. (1990). Feminist methodologies in criminology: A new approach or old wine in new bottles? In Loraine Gelsthorpe and Alison Morris (Eds.), *Feminist perspectives in criminology*. Philadelphia, PA: Open University Press.

Gelsthorpe, Loraine, & Morris, Alison (Eds.). (1990). *Feminist perspectives in criminology*. Philadelphia, PA: Open University Press.

Gilligan, Carol. (1982). *In a different voice: Psychological theory and women's development*. Cambridge, MA: Harvard University Press.

Giordano, Peggy, Kerbel, Sandra, & Dudley, Sandra. (1981). The economics of female criminality: An analysis of police blotters, 1890-1975. In Lee Bowker (Ed.), *Women and crime in America*. New York: Macmillan.

Glaser, Barney, & Strauss, Anselm. (1967). *The discovery of grounded theory: Strategies for qualitative research*. Chicago: Aldine.

Glenwick, David S. (1988). Community psychology perspectives on delinquency: An introduction to the special issue. *Criminal Justice and Behavior, 15*, 276–85.

Glueck, Sheldon, & Glueck, Eleanor. (1934). *Five hundred delinquent women*. New York: Knopf.

Gora, JoAnn Gennaro. (1982). *The new female criminal: Empirical reality or social myth?* New York: Praeger.

Gordon, Linda. (1988). *Heroes of their own lives: The politics and history of family violence.* New York: Viking.

Hagan, John, Simpson, John, & Gillis, A. (1979). The sexual stratification of social control: A gender-based perspective on crime and delinquency. *British Journal of Sociology, 30,* 25–38.

Harding, Sandra (Ed.). (1987). *Feminism and methodology.* Bloomington and Indianapolis: Open University Press.

Harris, Anthony. (1977). Sex and theories of deviance: Toward a functional theory of deviant type-scripts. *American Sociological Review, 42,* 3–16.

Harry, Bruce, & Balcer, Charlotte. (1987). Menstruation and crime: A critical review of the literature from the clinical criminology perspective. *Behavioral Sciences and the Law, 5,* 307–21.

Heidensohn, Frances. (1968). The deviance of women: A critique and an enquiry. *British Journal of Sociology, 19,* 160–75.

Heidensohn, Frances. (1985). *Women and crime.* London: Macmillan Education.

Heney, Jan. (1990). *Report on self-injurious behaviour in the Kingston Prison for Women.* Ottawa: Correctional Service of Canada.

Henson, S. Deon. (1980). Female as totem, female as taboo: An inquiry into the freedom to make connections. In Edward Sagarin (Ed.), *Taboos in criminology.* Beverly Hills, CA: Sage.

Hirschi, Travis. (1969). *Causes of delinquency.* Berkeley, CA: University of California Press.

Hoffman-Bustamente, Dale. (1973). The nature of female criminality. *Issues in Criminology, 8*(2), 117–36.

Horney, Julie. (1978). Menstrual cycles and criminal responsibility. *Law and Human Behavior, 2,* 25–36.

Hunt, David E. (1987). *Beginning with ourselves: In practice, theory, and human affairs.* Cambridge, MA: Brookline Books.

Hunt, David E. (1992). *The renewal of personal energy.* Toronto: OISE Press.

Jaggar, Alison. (1977). Male instructors, feminism, and women's studies. *Teaching Philosophy, 2,* 247–56.

James, Jennifer. (1976). Motivations for entrance into prostitution. In Laura Crites (Ed.), *The female offender.* Lexington, MA: D.C. Heath and Company.

James, Jennifer, & Thornton, William. (1980). Women's liberation and the female delinquent. *Journal of Research in Crime and Delinquency, 17,* 230–44.

Johnson, Holly. (1987). Getting the facts straight: A statistical overview. In E. Adelberg and C. Currie (Eds.), *Too few to count: Canadian women in conflict with the law.* Vancouver: Press Gang.

Johnson, Richard, Marcos, Anastasios, & Bahr, Stephen. (1987). The role of peers in the complex etiology of adolescent drug use. *Criminology, 25,* 323–40.

Jordan, Judith. (1985). Empathy and the mother–daughter relationship. In J. Jordan, J. Surrey, & A. Kaplan, *Women and empathy: Implications for psychological development and psychotherapy. Work in progress.* Stone Center Working Papers Series. Wellesley, MA: Stone Center.

Jordan, Judith. (1986). The meaning of mutuality. *Work in Progress.* Stone Center Working Papers Series. Wellesley, MA: Stone Center.

Jordan, Judith. (1991a). Empathy and self boundaries. In J. Jordan, A. Kaplan, J. Miller, I. Stiver, & J. Surrey (Eds.), *Women's growth in connection.* New York: Guilford Press.

Jordan, Judith. (1991b). Do you believe that the concepts of self and autonomy are useful in understanding women? In J.B. Miller, J.V. Jordan, A.G. Kaplan, I.P. Stiver, & J.L. Surrey, *Some misconceptions and reconceptions of a relational approach. Work in progress.* Stone Center Working Papers Series. Wellesley, MA: Stone Center.

Jordan, Judith, Surrey, Janet, & Kaplan, Alexandra. (1983). *Women and empathy: Implications for psychological development and psychotherapy. Work in progress.* Stone Center Working Papers Series. Wellesley, MA: Stone Center.

Kaplan, Alexandra. (1983). *Empathic communication in the psychotherapy relationship. Work in Progress.* Stone Center Working Papers Series. Wellesley, MA: Stone Center.

Kaplan, Alexandra. (1991). How can a group of white, heterosexual, privileged women claim to speak of 'women's' experience? In J.B. Miller, J.V. Jordan, A.G. Kaplan, I.P. Stiver, & J.L. Surrey. *Some misconceptions and reconceptions of a relational approach: Work in Progress.* Stone Center Working Papers Series. Wellesley, MA: Stone Center.

Kendall, Kathleen. (1993). *Literature review of therapeutic services for women in prison.* Ottawa: Correctional Service of Canada.

Kertzman, Don. (1980). *Dependency, frustration, tolerance and impulse control in child abusers.* Saratoga, CA: Century Twenty-One.

Kirby, Sandra, & McKenna, Kate. (1989). *Experience research social change: Methods from the margins.* Toronto: Garamond.

Kittay, E.F., & Meyers, D.T. (Eds.). (1987). *Women and moral theory.* New York: Rowman & Littlefield.

Klein, Dorie. (1973). The etiology of female crime: A review of the literature. *Issues in Criminology, 8*(2), 3–30.

Klein, Dorie, & Kress, June. (1976). Any woman's blues: A critical overview of women, crime, and the criminal justice system. *Crime and Social Justice, 5* (Spring–Summer), 34–49.

Kohlberg, Lawrence. (1981). *The philosophy of moral development*. San Francisco: Harper & Row.

Konopka, Gisela. (1966). *The adolescent girl in conflict*. Englewood Cliffs, NJ: Prentice-Hall.

Korbin, Jill. (1986). Childhood histories of women imprisoned for fatal child maltreatment. *Child Abuse and Neglect, 10*, 331–38.

LaPrairie, Carol. (1987). Native women and crime in Canada: A theoretical model. *Canadian Journal of Native Studies, 7*, 121–37.

Leahey, Thomas H. (1987). *A history of psychology: Main currents in psychological thought*. Englewood Cliffs, NJ: Prentice-Hall.

Leon, Irving G. (1986). Psychodynamics of perinatal loss. *Psychiatry, 49*, 312–24.

Leonard, E.B. (1982). *Women, crime, and society: A critique of criminology theory*. New York: Longman.

Lewis, Emanuel. (1976, September 18). The management of stillbirth: Coping with an unreality. *Lancet*, pp. 619–20.

Lewis, Emanuel, & Page, Anne. (1978). An overlooked catastrophe. *British Journal of Medical Psychology, 51*, 237–41.

Lincoln, Y.S., & Guba, E.G. (1985). *Naturalistic inquiry*. Beverly Hills, CA: Sage.

Lombroso, Caesar, & Ferrero, William. (1959). *The female offender*. London: Peter Owen. (Original work published 1895).

Lyons, Nona. (1983). Two perspectives on self, relationship, and morality. *Harvard Educational Review, 53*, 125–45.

Mann, Coramae Richey. (1984). *Female crime and delinquency*. Tuscaloosa, AL: University of Alabama Press.

Mathews, Fred. (1987). *Familiar strangers: A study of adolescent prostitution*. Toronto: Central Toronto Youth Services.

Mawby, Rob. (1980). Sex and crime: The results of a self-report study. *British Journal of Sociology, 31*, 525–43.

Mayer, Elizabeth. (1985). 'Everybody must be just like me': Observations on female castration anxiety. *International Journal of Psycho-Analysis, 66*, 331–47.

Melnick, B., & Hurley, J. (1969). Distinctive personality attributes of child-abusing mothers. *Journal of Consulting and Clinical Psychology, 33*, 746–9.

Merton, Robert K. (1938). Social structure and anomie. *American Sociological Review, 3*, 672–82.

Merton, Robert K. (1975). Social structure and anomie. In Stuart Traub & Craig Little (Eds.), *Theories of Deviance*. Itasca, IL: F.E. Peacock.

Miller, Alice. (1986). *Thou shalt not be aware: Society's betrayal of the child.* New York: New American Library.

Miller, Jean Baker. (1976). *Toward a new psychology of women.* Boston: Beacon Press.

Miller, Jean Baker. (1982). *Women and power. Work in progress.* Stone Center Working Papers Series. Wellesley, MA: Stone Center.

Miller, Jean Baker. (1984). The development of women's sense of self. *Work in progress.* Stone Center Working Papers Series. Wellesley, MA: Stone Center.

Miller, Jean Baker. (1986). *What do we mean by relationships? Work in progress.* Stone Center Working Paper Series. Wellesley, MA: Stone Center.

Miller, Jean Baker. (1988). *Connections, disconnections and violations. Work in progress.* Stone Center Working Papers Series. Wellesley, MA: Stone Center.

Miller, S.M. (1952). The participant observer and 'Over-Rapport'. *American Sociological Review, 17,* 97–8.

Morris, Allison. (1987). *Women, crime and criminal justice.* Oxford: Basil Blackwell.

Morris, Allison, and Gelsthorpe, Loraine. (1981). False clues and female crime. In Allison Morris and Loraine Gelsthorpe (Eds.), *Women and crime: Papers presented to the Cropwood Round-Table Conference, December, 1980.* Cropwood Conference Series no. 13. Cambridge, UK.

Morris, Allison, and Gelsthorpe, Loraine. (1991). Feminist perspectives in criminology: Transforming and transgressing. *Women and Criminal Justice, 2*(2), 3–23.

Morris, Ruth. (1964). Female delinquency and relational problems. *Social Forces, 43,* 82–9.

Moustakas, Clark. (1977). *Turning points.* Englewood Cliffs, NJ: Prentice-Hall.

Mukherjee, Satyanshu, and Fitzgerald, William. (1981). The myth of rising female crime. In S. Mukherjee & J. Scutt (Eds.), *Women and crime.* Sydney, Australia: George Allen & Unwin.

Mukherjee, S.K., & Scutt, J.A. (Eds.). (1981). *Women and crime.* Sydney, Australia: George Allen & Unwin.

Naffine, Ngaire. (1981). Theorizing about female crime. In S. Mukherjee & J. Scutt (Eds.), *Women and crime.* Sydney, Australia: George Allen & Unwin.

Naffine, Ngaire. (1987). *Female crime: The construction of women in criminology.* Sydney, Australia: George Allen & Unwin.

Naffine, Ngaire, & Gale, Fay. (1989). Testing the nexus: Crime, gender, and unemployment. *British Journal of Criminology, 29,* 144–55.

Noddings, Nell. (1984) *Caring: A feminine approach to ethics and moral education.* Berkeley, CA: University of California Press.

Norlan, Stephen, Wessel, Randall, & Shover, Neal. (1981). Masculinity and delinquency. *Criminology, 19*, 421–33.

Oakley, Anne. (1981). Interviewing women: A contradiction in terms. In H. Roberts (Ed.), *Doing feminist research*. London: Routledge & Kegan Paul.

Parsons, Talcott. (1949). *Essays in sociological theory*. Glencoe, IL: Free Press.

Pollak, Otto. (1950). *The criminality of women*. New York: A.S. Barnes.

Prins, Herschel. (1982). *Criminal behaviour: An introduction to criminology and the penal system*. London: Tavistock.

Rasche, Christine. (1974). The female offender as an object of criminological research. *Criminal Justice and Behavior, 1*, 301–20.

Ray, JoAnn, and Briar, Katherine. (1988). Economic motivators for shoplifting. *Journal of Sociology & Social Welfare, 15*, 177–89.

Redl, Fritz, and Toch, Hans. (1979). The psychoanalytic perspective. In Hans Toch (Ed.), *Psychology of crime and criminal justice*. New York: Holt, Rinehart and Winston.

Reinharz, Shulamit. (1979). *On becoming a social scientist: From survey research and participant observation to experiential analysis*. San Francisco: Jossey-Bass.

Reinharz, Shulamit. (1983). Experiential analysis: A contribution to feminist research. In G. Bowles and R.D. Klein (Eds.), *Theories of women's studies*. New York: Routledge.

Rice, Marcia. (1990). Challenging orthodoxies in feminist theory: A Black feminist critique. In Loraine Gelsthorpe and Alison Morris (Eds.), *Feminist perspectives in criminology*. Philadelphia, PA: Open University Press.

Rivera, Margo. (1991). *Multiple personality: An outcome of child abuse*. Toronto: Education/Dissociation.

Ross, Robert, & Fabiano, Elizabeth. (1985). *Time to think: A cognitive model of delinquency prevention and rehabilitation*. Ottawa: Institute of Social Sciences and Arts.

Schon, Donald. (1983). *The reflective practitioner: How professionals think in action*. New York: Basic Books.

Scutt, Jocelynne. (1978). Debunking theory of female 'masked' criminal. *Australia and New Zealand Journal of Criminology, 11*, 23–42.

Shaw, Margaret, with Rodgers, Karen, Blanchette, Johanne, Hattem, Tina, Thomas, Lee Seto, & Tamarack, Lada. (1990). *Survey of federally sentenced women: Report to the Task Force on the Prison Survey*. Ottawa: Ministry of the Solicitor General of Canada.

Shaw, Margaret, with Rodgers, Karen, Blanchette, Johanne, Hattem, Tina, Thomas, Lee Seto, & Tamarack, Lada. (1991). *Paying the price: Federally sentenced women in context*. Ottawa: Ministry of the Solicitor General of Canada.

Sherif, Carolyn Wood. (1987). Bias in psychology. In Sandra Harding (Ed.), *Feminism and methodology*. Indianapolis, IN: Indiana University Press.

Shoalts, David. (1991, June 11). Ending bias in justice system conference goal. *The Globe and Mail*, p. A6.

Silman, Janet. (1987). *Enough is enough: Aboriginal women speak out*. Toronto: Women's Press.

Simon, Rita. (1975). *Women and crime*. Toronto: Lexington Books.

Simon, Rita, & Landis, Jean. (1991). *The crimes women commit, the punishments they receive*. Toronto: Lexington Books.

Simons, Ronald, Miller, Martin, & Aigner, Stephen. (1980). Contemporary theories of deviance and female delinquency: An empirical test. *Journal of Research in Crime and Delinquency, 17*, 42–57.

Simpson, Sally. (1989). Feminist theory, crime, and justice. *Criminology, 27*, 605–30.

Smart, Carol. (1976). *Women, crime and criminology: A feminist critique*. London: Routledge & Kegan Paul.

Smart, Carol. (1990). Feminist approaches to criminology, or postmodern woman meets atavistic man. In Loraine Gelsthorpe and Alison Morris (Eds.), *Feminist perspectives in criminology*. Philadelphia, PA: Open University Press.

Smith, Dorothy E. (1986). *The social organization of knowledge*. Ontario Institute for Studies in Education. Toronto: Author.

Smith, Douglas. (1979). Sex and deviance: An assessment of major sociological variables. *The Sociological Quarterly, 20*, 183–95.

Spradley, J.P. (1979). *The ethnographic interview*. New York: Holt, Rinehart and Winston.

Steele, Brandt, & Pollock, Carl. (1974). A psychiatric study of parents who abuse infants and small children. In Ray E. Helfer and C. Henry Kempe (Eds.), *The battered child*. Chicago, IL: University of Chicago Press.

Steffensmeier, Darrell. (1981). Crime and the contemporary woman: An analysis of changing levels of female property crime, 1960–1975. In Lee Bowker (Ed.), *Women and crime in America*. New York: Macmillan.

Stiver, Irene. (1986). *Beyond the Oedipus complex: Mothers and daughters. Work in Progress*. Stone Center Working Papers Series. Wellesley, MA: Stone Center.

Stiver, Irene. (1990). *Dysfunctional families and wounded relationships. Work in progress* (Parts 1 and 2). Stone Center Working Papers Series. Wellesley, MA: Stone Center.

Straus, Murray A., Gelles, Richard J., & Steinmetz, S. (1980). *Behind closed doors: Violence in the American family*. New York: Doubleday.

Sullivan, Edmund V. (1984). *A critical psychology*. New York: Plenum.

Surrey, Janet. (1984). *Self-in-relation: A theory of women's development. Work in progress.* Stone Center Working Papers Series. Wellesley, MA: Stone Center.

Surrey, Janet. (1985). *The relational self in women: Clinical implications. Work in progress.* Stone Center Working Papers Series. Wellesley, MA: Stone Center.

Surrey, Janet. (1987). *Relationship and empowerment. Work in progress.* Stone Center Working Papers Series. Wellesley, MA: Stone Center.

Surrey, Janet. (1990). Empathy: Evolving theoretical perspectives. In J.L. Surrey, A.G. Kaplan, & J.V. Jordan, *Empathy revisited: Work in progress.* Stone Center Working Papers Series. Wellesley, MA: Stone Center.

Sutherland, Edwin, & Cressey, Donald. (1966). *Principles of Criminology* (7th ed.). Philadelphia, PA: J.B. Lippincott.

Tavris, Carol. (1989). *Anger: The misunderstood emotion.* New York: Simon & Schuster.

Taylor, S., & Bogdan, R. (1984). *Introduction to qualitative research methods: The search for meanings.* New York: John Wiley & Sons.

Terry, Robert. (1979). Trends in female crime: A comparison of Adler, Simon, and Steffensmeier. *California Sociologist, 2,* 200–12.

Thomas, William I. (1923). *The unadjusted girl: With cases and standpoint for behaviour analysis.* Montclair, NJ: Patterson Smith.

Traub, Stuart, & Little, Craig (Eds.). (1975). *Theories of Deviance.* Itasca, IL: F.E. Peacock.

Turner, Clevonne. (1985). *Psychosocial barriers to Black women's career development. Work in Progress.* Stone Center Working Papers Series. Wellesley, MA: Stone Center.

Valverde, Mariana. (1991). Feminist perspectives on criminology. In Jane Gladstone, Richard Ericson, & Clifford Shearing (Eds.), *Criminology: A reader's guide.* Toronto: Centre of Criminology, University of Toronto.

Vienneau, David. (1991, June 11) 'Dog-eat-dog' policies called threat to women. *The Toronto Star.*

Walker, Lenore E. (1989). *Terrifying love: Why battered women kill and how society responds.* New York: Harper & Row.

Warren, Marguerite, & Hindelang, Michael. (1979). Current explanations of offender behavior. In Hans Toch (Ed.), *Psychology of crime and criminal justice.* New York: Holt, Rinehart and Winston.

Webber, Marlene, & McGilvary, Tony. (1988). *Square John: A true story.* Toronto: University of Toronto Press.

Weisheit, Ralph. (1984). Women and crime: Issues and perspectives. *Sex Roles, 11,* 567–81.

Weisheit, Ralph, & Mahan, Sue. (1988). *Women, crime, and criminal justice.* Cincinnati, OH: Anderson.

Widom, Cathy. (1981). Perspectives of female criminality: A critical examination of assumptions. In Allison Morris and Loraine Gelsthorpe (Eds.), *Women and crime: Papers presented to the Cropwood Round-Table Conference, December, 1980.* Cropwood Conference Series No. 13. Cambridge, UK.

Wiehe, Vernon. (1985). Empathy and locus of control in child abusers. *Journal of Social Service Research, 9,* 2–3 17–30.

Williams, Juanita. (1983). *Psychology of women: Behavior in a biosocial context.* New York: W.W. Norton.

Windschuttle, E. (1981). Women, crime and punishment. In S. Mukherjee & J. Scutt (Eds.), *Women and crime.* Sydney, Australia: George Allen & Unwin.

Wine, Jeri D. (1983). Gynocentric values and feminist psychology. In A. Miles and G. Finn (Eds.), *Feminism in Canada: From pressure to politics.* Montreal: Black Rose Books.

Worrall, Anne. (1990). *Offending women: Female lawbreakers and the criminal justice system.* London: Routledge.

Yalom, Irving. (1980). *Existential psychotherapy.* New York: Basic Books.

Yochelson, S., & Samenow, S.E. (1976). *The criminal personality.* New York: Jason Aronson.

York, Geoffrey. (1989). *The dispossessed: Life and death in Native Canada.* Toronto: Lester & Orpen Dennys.

Zeanah, Charles. (1989). Adaptation following perinatal loss: A critical review. *Journal of the American Academy of Child and Adolescent Psychiatry, 28,* 467–80.

Index

Abrahamsen, David, 16
abuse: of children, 28, 51, 90–1; denial of, 115; fatal, 104, 106, 109; by nuns, 89; of parent, 60; by peers or partners, 51, 89, 93; precipitated by injury to the abuser, 130; of self, 67, 92, 132, 146n; sexual, 34, 49, 72, 90, 134; by siblings, 102–3; of siblings, 34; witnessed, 26, 29–30, 35, 58–9, 60, 64, 68, 101–2, 109. *See also* disconnection; violence
addiction. *See* alcohol, drugs
Adelberg, Ellen, 41
Adler, Freda, 19, 20
adoption, 88–9
alcohol, 64; parents'/grandparents' use of, 26–7, 55, 64, 76, 83, 95; partner's use of, 91, 93; women's use of, 53, 56, 65, 69, 77, 84, 93, 95, 113
Allen, Judith, 128
anger, 85–6, 89, 92, 105, 108–9, 112, 113, 114, 117; and alcohol, 79, 91; cultural issues surrounding, 79, 81; and lawbreaking, 98; in lieu of other feelings, 76, 78, 79,

80, 86, 87, 88, 94, 109; as a secondary emotion, 79, 81, 97, 133; unpoliticized, 82
Arlene, 25, 29–31, 36, 37, 38, 39, 40, 42, 43, 112, 116, 126

Becker, H., 145n
Bell, Quentin, 122
Bernardez, Teresa, 81
bias. *See* researcher bias
Bishop, Cecil, 19
Bonnie, 47, 48–53, 71, 74, 113, 116, 134
Brown, Stephanie, 74
Brownmiller, Susan, 20

Caplan, Paula, 42, 43, 79, 109, 133
Carlen, Pat, 21, 41, 42, 130
Chesler, Phyllis, 20
Chesney-Lind, Meda , 20
child abuse. *See* abuse, of children
child support. *See* socioeconomic status
confirmability, of qualitative studies, 140, 142
connection in relationships: through drugs and alcohol, 73, 74; as it fur-

poverty: Anne Worrall's definition of, 125; as the cause of women's crime, 21–2, 41–2

power: to change, 131; definition of, 117–18; false, 120, 123; of others, over women, 39–41; as protection, 105

psychological development of women, 10; and childbirth and loss of children, 51, 57, 69, 84, 106–8. *See also* relational development theory

racism, 44

relational development theory, 10–12, 42, 52, 72, 110, 112, 114, 124; relevance to men, 128

relationships, 112, 113, 114, 115–16; centrality to women's lives, 111; and empowerment, 10, 118, 120; loss of, 112; maintaining appearance of, 116; violence as interference with, 130

research: 'design,' 137; directions, 135; 'grand tour' question, 144n; interpretation as a component of, 9–10, 144n; participant observation, 137, 141, 150n; rigour of, 85; synthesis and analysis in, 138–9, 149n; underlying principles, 137–8; as a vehicle of growth, 12–13. *See also* criminology of women, participants

researcher bias, 8, 15–16; and limitations of Stone Center group, 11

role theory, 16, 18–19, 20

role-frustration, 18

Rose, 25, 31–3, 36, 37, 38, 39, 43, 112, 116

Ross, Robert, 118, 119

Sarah, 47, 62–7, 71, 74, 75, 113, 116

self-boundaries, 72

separation: and individuation, 123, 128–9, 148n; as a way of organizing society, 14–15

sexual abuse. *See* abuse, sexual

Sherif, Carolyn Wood, 9

Simon, Rita, 17, 19, 20

Slater, Eliot, 16–17

Smart, Carol, 18, 20

social class: and family values, 26, 28, 36, 37–8, 39; link to crime, 41–2; social expectations, 43, 45–6

social learning theory, 108

socioeconomic status: and child support, 25, 27, 33, 37, 38; and earning power, 39–40; and the impact of children, 42–3

Stiver, Irene, 10, 72, 73, 115

Stone Center, 10, 11, 114

strain theory. *See* Merton, Robert K.

subjective accounts: value of, 4, 125; verification of, 12. *See also* trustworthiness, establishing

Surrey, Janet, 10, 119

Sutherland, Edwin, 15, 145n

Task Force on Federally Sentenced Women, 130, 133

Thomas, William I., 16

Thornton, William, 20

transferability, of qualitative studies, 140, 141, 149n

triangulation, 141, 150n

trustworthiness, establishing, 140–2, 149n

Turner, Clevonne, 44

unemployment, effects of, 28, 61